Toss the Rocks and Get on With It!

Toss the Rocks and Get on With It!

Don't Let Your Past Determine Your Future

Donna Strong

Published by
Hybrid Global Publishing
333 E 14th Street
#3C
New York, NY 10003

Copyright © 2024 by Donna Strong

All rights reserved. No part of this book may be reproduced or transmitted in any form or by any means, electronic or mechanical, including photocopying, recording, or by any information storage and retrieval system, without the written permission of the Publisher, except where permitted by law.

Manufactured in the United States of America, or in the United Kingdom when distributed elsewhere.

Strong, Donna
Toss the Rocks and Get on With It! Don't Let Your Past Determine Your Future
    ISBN: 978-1-961757-71-4
    eBook: 978-1-961757-72-1

LCCN: 2024924748

Cover design by: Julia Kuris
Copyediting by: Sue Toth
Interior design by: Suba Murugan
Author photo by: Clix North Atlanta Photography
Website: www.tosstherocks.com

This book is dedicated to my sweet mother who told me I was going to write a book. She did not know what kind of book but said I would "figure it out." She was right! I thank her for being the catalyst that led me on this journey.

Acknowledgments

Thanks to:

My wonderful husband, Murray, for all his help, support, and encouragement.

My amazing daughter, Katie, for her support and encouraging words.

My parents, who made me who I am today.

Kelly Brumbeloe, pastor at Embrace, for her riveting sermon on the Holy Spirit.

The Holy Spirit who boldly and clearly told me to write this book.

Lynn Hanna, my dear friend, who is a motivator and supporter.

Tonya Leary, my neighbor and special friend, who cheers me on.

Claudia Volkman, my editor, for her creativity, knowledge, and positivity.

Natalie Birnbaum, my friend and neighbor, for giving generously of her time to proofread my book.

Mike Birnbaum for his talented, creative photography and invaluable technical assistance.

All the numerous friends who encourage and believe in me.

Contents

Acknowledgments vii

Introduction 1

Part 1: Rocks? What Rocks? 7
Step One: Assess Your Current Situation 9
Step Two: Envision Your Ideal Life 19
Step Three: Become Aware 31
Step Four: Count the Cost 41

Part 2: Get Rid of the Rocks Already! 47
Step Five: Toss the Rocks 49
    Lose the Fear 49
    Drop the Insecurity and Self-Doubt 58
    Free Yourself of Perfectionism 70
    Stop the People-Pleasing 79
    Let Go of Resentments 88
    Overcome Addictions 96

Part 3: The Time to Act Is NOW 105
Step Six: Develop Your Personal Action Plan 107

Conclusion 117

Introduction

The purpose of this book is to help you find joy by letting go of your emotional baggage. Imagine that you are carrying a bucket throughout your life. In this bucket are the negative things that hold you back and prevent you from getting to where you really want to be in life. In this book, these negative things are represented by rocks. Everybody has a bucket, and everybody has rocks!

These rocks represent old negative patterns of thinking, feeling, and behaving that don't serve you well. They are obstacles to your true happiness and joy. They represent who you do not want to be anymore.

In order to achieve your best life, you will need to become aware of your rocks, decide to toss them, and take action to move toward your joy. At the end of your life, I want each of you to be able to say, "It was a great ride," vs "I wish I would have." This book will help you get there.

WHY I WROTE THIS BOOK

My mother was in the late stages of Alzheimer's and had a very vivid imagination. She kept talking for months about a book she needed to return to the owner, but she couldn't figure out who it belonged to. One day, in a clear state of mind, she told me that she had figured out the book dilemma. She went on to tell me with great certainty that *I was to write a book*! I was bewildered as I've never considered myself a writer.

"What kind of book, Mama?" I asked her.

"A children's book," she replied.

"What kind of children's book? A book for children or for parents raising children?"

After a few moments, she said, "I don't know, but you will figure it out."

About a year later, in March 2010, my sweet Mama passed away. In her mind, she had solved the book puzzle, and she never mentioned it again.

For years, the idea of writing a book tugged at me. Fear and busyness kept me from writing the book, until now. You see, my number-one issue has always been FEAR. But finally, after many years, I came to believe that I must write this book. As for who the "children" are, they are each one of you who chooses to read this book. We are ALL children of God!

My own bucket in life has been heavy with emotional baggage, which I call "rocks," and I have had to learn ways to "toss the rocks" so they didn't continue to cripple my life. I often wished I would have had someone to "coach" me on how to do this.

At 30 years old, I was a wreck. I looked great on the outside with my youth, corporate job, sports car, money in the bank, and active social life. I had moved from my small hometown in North Carolina to Atlanta and looked the part of a successful young female. But inside, I was miserable and didn't know how to change my life. I desperately wanted a relationship, a family, and a job that I enjoyed, but I clearly was not moving in that direction. To fill up the holes, I became a workaholic, partied too much, drank too much, and dated all the wrong men. Why? Because the rocks in my bucket were so big that I really didn't know how to toss them, and I wasn't even aware of all of them. I didn't understand how they got there in the first place, and I was clueless how to overcome them. I was in therapy, but I didn't feel I was getting at the true issues. My rocks at age thirty included many fears, such as the fear of:

- getting married
- having children

- quitting things
- failure
- not being good enough
- letting someone down
- being cheated on again
- loss of parents

I also struggled with some other big rocks:

- lack of self-love
- self-doubt
- resentments

These "rocks," especially my fears, controlled my life. Fortunately, I was able to toss many of these rocks. I finally married an incredible man at age 39, and I can't imagine life without him. We have an awesome daughter who we adopted when I was in my forties. She is an incredible gift and I absolutely love being a mom. Yes, I was "late to the party" due to all the fears I had to address, but I got there.

Daily, I still work to overcome fears and ensure they are not controlling my life. I now know what my rocks are, how they got there, and what I need to do to toss them, so they don't ruin the rest of my life. I have learned that I must not allow my past fears and issues to determine my future. I know what I need to do in order to find my joy in life.

My goal is to "give back" to others what I have learned on my journey. I have a burning passion to reach out and help others make their lives more joyful and fulfilling. I want each of you to understand that whatever happened to you in your past does not have to dictate your future. Thank you for reading this book—may it help you immensely.

THE SIX STEPS FOR LIVING A LIFE OF JOY

In our journey together, we will cover the following six steps:

Step One: Assess Your Current Situation
You will determine the areas of your life which are not serving you well. These are the things that you want to change.

Step Two: Envision Your Ideal Life
You will define what your ideal life of joy looks like.

Step Three: Become Aware
You will uncover the real rocks in your bucket that are preventing you from moving from your current situation to your ideal life.

Step Four: Count the Cost
You will look at what it is costing you to continue carrying the rocks in your bucket vs. tossing them.

Step Five: Toss the Rocks
This step covers strategies for getting rid of your rocks. It's the "HOW" piece. Six of the most common "rocks" will be addressed:

- Fear
- Insecurity and Self-Doubt
- Perfectionism
- People-Pleasing
- Resentments
- Addictions

Step Six: Develop Your Personal Action Plan
You will develop a personal action plan that will enable you to move from your current situation to your ideal life.

YOUR JOURNEY

As you go through this book and look at your own rocks, don't expect yourself to be perfect. Rocks will always fill your bucket based on what is going on in your life. There is always a gap between where you are in life and where you want to be. This is how we grow. My hope is that you will learn to identify and toss your rocks on an ongoing basis, so they do not control you in a negative way.

Remember, we are all works in progress. My sincere hope for you is that you will empty that heavy bucket and experience true joy in your life.

My intent with this book is to be your coach, your partner on this fascinating journey. I want this to be YOUR story and focus on how you can improve your life so you can have a truly joyful life. This book is not just for reading, but also for DOING. You'll want to do the personal exercises to achieve your best results. Consider it your own personal guidebook. You are worth the time! You give of yourself to so many other people and activities. Now it's time for YOU! It's time to find YOUR joy!

Part 1

Rocks? What Rocks?

Part 1 will cover the first four of the six steps I've identified to toss the rocks that are holding you back and finally start living the life of joy you deserve. You will take an introspective look at:

Step One: Assess your Current Situation (what areas of your life are not working)

Step Two: Envision Your Ideal Life (what would a joyful life really look like)

Step Three: Become Aware (of the rocks that are holding you back)

Step Four: Count the Cost (of not tossing your rocks)

Step One

Assess Your Current Situation

> *The greatest discovery one can make is not external, but internal--facing the mirror of discontent with unflinching honesty. It is in the depths of self-awareness that the seeds of true happiness are sown.*
> —Albert Einstein

In this chapter, we will look at the areas of your life which are not working in ways that serve you well. You will determine the things that are causing you pain, dissatisfaction, unhappiness, or anger. This exercise of identifying what is not working is a critical step towards making positive changes.

When I ask people how their life is going, usually they say, "Fine." It's much like asking a person, "How are you doing today?" Most people say fine even though they may be falling apart inside. "I'm fine" is a standard response that somewhere along the way, we've been taught to say. And it's often not the truth.

While it is acceptable not to tell others your business, it is not okay to be dishonest with yourself. Only by looking deep inside and being brutally honest can we impact changes within ourselves which lead to a more joyful life.

When I was in my thirties, I looked great on the outside. However, I was like a microwave: I was shiny on the outside, but if you opened the door, I was a mess inside. I hid my pain by becoming a workaholic and partying too much. I would always rationalize that I would make changes "later." But in reality, I was terrified of making changes and decisions. I wasn't even sure what the problem was, which crippled my ability to make changes.

To get the most out of this book, I want you to make an honest deep dive into what is not optimal in your life. I have found that it is helpful to look at each of the main areas of our lives, and drill down to see if there are areas of discontent within each category.

The following exercise is designed to help you discover any areas of dissatisfaction. This is the DOING portion. If you skip this, you are just cheating yourself.

WHAT'S NOT WORKING WELL:

1. **Health (Nutrition and Fitness)**
   Are you getting enough exercise? Eating a healthy diet? Happy with your weight? Are there any doctor appointments or medical procedures you are putting off?

   _____
   _____
   _____
   _____
   _____
   _____
   _____

2. **Career**
   Do you enjoy your work? Like the people you work with? Feel you are using your strengths and talents? Have a path for advancement? Satisfied with the amount of money you are making? Are you a "quiet quitter" or are you passionate about your work?

   _____
   _____

3. Spiritual Life

Do you believe there is a power greater than yourself? Do you know why you are here? What your purpose is? Are there areas of your spiritual life that you would like to explore or learn more about? How do you find peace in your daily life?

4. Family Life

How is your relationship with your spouse or significant other, your children, parents, siblings, and extended family members? If you are single, are you happy? Do you spend enough quality time with those important to you?

5. **Relationships with Friends**

    Do you have a close friend (s) with whom you can be open and honest? Do you have a circle of friends that you enjoy spending time with? Do you have any toxic relationships that you need to re-think?

6. **Financial Health**

    Are you comfortable with the amount you are saving for retirement, major purchases, college education for your children? Are you living paycheck to paycheck? Feeling stressed about money? Have too much credit card debt?

7. Work/Life Balance

Are you happy with your current work/life balance? Does your job spill over and negatively impact your personal life or health? Do you prioritize time for those important to you and for activities you enjoy?

8. Emotional Health

Are you at peace? Do you find it difficult to manage certain emotions effectively? Are you depressed? Are you carrying emotional baggage from your past that is impacting your happiness?

9. **Recreation/Fun Time**

   Are you happy with the amount of fun and recreational time you have in your life? Are there new hobbies, sports, or activities you would like to explore?

   _____
   _____
   _____
   _____
   _____
   _____

10. **Personal Growth**

    Are you learning new things? Are there any skills or education you would like to further develop? Are there self-limiting beliefs that hinder your progress?

    _____
    _____
    _____
    _____
    _____
    _____

Now, it's time to summarize your overall current state. Here are a few examples to get you going:

Assess Your Current Situation

Example 1: Current State (Overwhelmed)
- High anxiety
- Poor work/life balance
- Fear of making mistakes
- Perfectionism, resulting in slowness and inaction
- Feeling out-of-control/overwhelmed
- Lack of exercise
- Not eating healthy foods
- Life not headed in desired direction

Example 2: Current State (Depressed)
- Depressed
- Too thin
- Sleep too late in mornings
- Burdened with worry
- No interest in doing anything
- Not physically fit
- No purpose in life

Example 3: Current State (Financial Instability)
- Living paycheck to paycheck
- Credit card debt
- Too much impulse buying
- Hiding the depth of the problem from my spouse
- Feel like I am on a treadmill
- Lack of self-care
- Drinking too much

Your Turn!
Summarize your current situation below:

_____

_____

_____

_____

_____

_____

_____

_____

_____

_____

_____

_____

_____

_____

_____

_____

Great job! Next, you will describe the life you want to be living, one that is full of joy. Remember, you are not stuck in your current situation. Each of us has the CHOICE to change the things that are within our control.

There are two types of circumstances: things we can change and things we cannot change. We can't change the past, someone else's thoughts, the weather, your family and background, or the traffic. To worry about these things and try to control them is a waste of time. In this book, we will focus on things we CAN change. Remember that you always have a choice to stay stuck or to make changes. The Serenity Prayer states this concept well:

> *God, grant me the serenity to accept the things I cannot change,*
> *The courage to change the things I can,*
> *And the wisdom to know the difference.*

KEY TAKEAWAYS

- You must clearly understand your current situation before you can move forward.
- Honesty with yourself is critical.
- You are not stuck! You can make the CHOICE to move forward.

Step Two

Envision Your Ideal Life

Begin with the end in mind.
—Stephen Covey

For approximately fourteen years of my career with IBM, I worked in personal development and sales training. As part of our curricula, we offered a class on Stephen Covey's book *The 7 Habits of Highly Effective People*. Years after attending the class and reading the book, the one habit that I used most often was "Begin with the end in mind."

By starting with a clear picture of what your ideal life of joy looks like, you can ensure that you focus on the things that are truly important to you. Covey points out that it is easy to get caught up in the busyness of life. You can be so busy climbing the ladder of success that you discover too late that it's leaning against the wrong wall.

Consider a person who has dedicated their life to achieving business and financial success, only to realize that their marriage has crumbled, and they don't really have a close relationship with their children. In the end, they feel empty and full of regret. Don't let this be you!

In this chapter, you will define what your ideal life of joy looks like. This introspective process is well worth your dedicated time and effort. Now is the time to silence your phone, get off social media, and spend some time in a quiet place.

When I ask people, "What would bring you joy," most people cannot clearly answer this question. It's a simple question, but many of us never take the time to really think about this. How much time have you given to getting clear on your destination? Now is the time!

As you complete the following exercises, relax and let your mind flow. Nothing is too silly to dream about if it brings you joy. It doesn't matter what other people think. There's no judging here. It is all about YOU and what personally makes *you* happy. But be aware: We all have a "Gremlin" that sits on our shoulder and whispers things in our ear such as:

- "You can't do that!"
- "That is a crazy idea!"
- "What would others think?"
- "What if I fail?"

You get the picture.

Now is the time to knock that Negative Nelly gremlin off your shoulder. Remember, no judging. You are brainstorming and dreaming in these exercises. Here we go!

THE DEEP DOWN AND HONEST EXERCISE

Answer each of these questions, which are designed to help you discover what your ideal state of a joyful life looks like:

1. If money were no object, what would you be doing?

_____

_____

_____

_____

_____

_____

_____

Envision Your Ideal Life

2. Look at your past. What were the five most joyful times in your life? What were you doing, and with whom?

_____
_____
_____
_____
_____
_____
_____

3. What motivates you to get out of bed in the morning, excited to start the day?

_____
_____
_____
_____
_____
_____
_____

4. What activities make you lose track of time because you enjoy them so much?

_____
_____
_____

5. Think back to your childhood. What did you enjoy doing?

6. What activities leave you feeling energized and alive rather than drained?

7. If you knew you could not fail, what would you be doing?

_____
_____
_____
_____
_____
_____
_____
_____

8. What are you doing when you feel a strong sense of purpose in life?

_____
_____
_____
_____
_____
_____
_____
_____

9. What hobbies, interests, or activities do you naturally love to do?

_____
_____
_____
_____

_____
_____
_____
_____

10. Picture your ideal day. What are you doing?

_____
_____
_____
_____
_____
_____
_____

11. Reflect on the above questions. Do you see a pattern?

_____
_____
_____
_____
_____
_____
_____
_____

I particularly find that Question 5 about our childhood can provide valuable insights. As children, we often engage in activities purely for the fun of it. These activities bring us joy. As adults, we often get so tied up in the busyness of life that we forget about making time for joy.

When I was a child, there were a number of kids in my neighborhood, and we played together almost every day. We rode bikes, played kickball, and kick the can. It was a different world back then when kids could play outdoors safely.

I also played indoors with my best friend and her younger sister, who lived next-door. We played "dolls," Barbies, and pretended we were teachers. We set up a classroom in their basement, complete with a blackboard, chairs, and desks. The hours flew by as we interacted with each other and simply played.

I also loved going to our lake cabin with my mom, dad, and brother. Often other relatives joined us, or I brought a girlfriend. We spent many happy hours fishing, boating, skiing, and floating in the lake on our "tubes." When I take a reflective look at what brings me joy as an adult, I realize that outdoor activities and the beauty of nature, along with spending time with family and friends still bring me much joy.

My daughter is an avid runner. When she was home for Christmas this year, I decided to join her on her run on the trail of her old high school. She ran, and I walked. About ten minutes into my walk, I was in awe. I was mesmerized by nature. I was surrounded by trees and found such peace among the birds, squirrels, the smell of the earth, and the flowing stream. Memories of walking my grandfather's farm as a child flooded my mind. I realized how much I had missed nature. I had been too busy with life to slow down and think about the things that had brought me joy in my past. Now, walking the trail and enjoying all that nature has to offer is one of my new hobbies!

Find time to engage in YOUR childhood joys! It's a matter of giving yourself full permission to take the time to enjoy life. What a great gift to give yourself!

I have one additional exercise that I have found to be insightful and useful over the years. I know I'm throwing a lot of assessments at you right now, but I know they can help you, so please make the time to complete these.

LOVES AND DISLIKES EXERCISE

This is a simple exercise that can yield interesting insights. Take ten minutes to really think through what you really LOVE to do, and what you truthfully DISLIKE doing. Do a brain dump and list as many things as you can. Work quickly and don't analyze—just get them on paper.

Be as specific as possible. Don't list something vague like "relaxing." Be specific and list what helps you relax—for example, massages, scented candles, listening to calming music, beautiful flowers, or being alone in your "girl/man cave."

Ready? GO!

THINGS I LOVE DOING	THINGS I DISLIKE DOING

Reflecting on your answers, ask yourself three questions:

1. How many of your "LOVE DOING" activities do you do daily?

2. How many of the "DISLIKE" activities are you doing?

3. What patterns do you see?

I recently completed this exercise again myself. I was amazed at how many "LOVES" I was not consistently doing, and how many "DISLIKES" I was giving into. My character defect of people-pleasing was influencing me to do things I didn't really want to do because it makes someone else happy! While making others happy is important, we should not short-change ourselves by allowing pleasing others to dominate our lives.

I enjoy hearing stories of people who have moved from a current situation that was not optimal to one that is fun and full of joy.

I have always loved the story of Bob Pranga, "Dr. Christmas." I first learned about Bob from a friend of mine, Rick Tamlyn, author of *Play Your Bigger Game*. Bob was Rick's first coaching client and had turned to Rick years ago because he was feeling lost. I interviewed Bob recently, and he agreed that I could share his story with you. It is one of inspiration!

Bob grew up in the Midwest, then moved to Manhattan. He worked at Macy's Herald Square in the holiday décor department. Macy's asked Bob to decorate the traditional Christmas tree, which is a big attraction for the store. It was so beautiful that many people complimented him, including the actress, Mia Farrow. This brought Bob joy, but he didn't act on it at the time.

Next, he moved to LA because he wanted to be an actor. He was told there were one hundred people who looked just like him and that he likely would get more work when he got older. At the time, he was more than $150k in debt. Out of desperation, he began working at a Christmas store in one of the malls.

Bob had always loved Christmas, and he decided he would create a career out of Christmas decorating. His decision was based on his realization that he only wanted to do work that was fun to him, and he wanted to have the ability to manage his own schedule. Bob established a brand along with his fellow actor, Debi Staron, called Dr. Christmas, Tree Stylist to the Stars, and began building his business one celebrity's house at a time.

Today he is well known in Hollywood, and over the last forty years, he has decorated the houses of many stars, including John Legend, Mariah Carey, Beyoncé, Steven Spielberg, Paris Hilton, Christina Aguilera, Kevin Hart, and Kris Jenner.

While he is now a huge success, Bob had his own "rocks" to toss in order to find true joy. He heard many "shoulds" as a child, such as "You should get a good job," or "you are no good." He had to overcome that parental tape that defined what a "good" job looked like. He also felt his weight was a disadvantage. He told himself that he was too fat to be successful. He also had issues with money, fearing that "I'll never have enough." He now realizes that money is simply something that gives him freedom.

Bob said his only regret is that he didn't toss his own "rocks" earlier. But he got there and created a world for himself that brings him happiness and joy. And so can YOU!!

YOUR TURN!

List Below What Your Ideal Life Looks Like:

_____

_____

_____

_____

_____

_____

_____

_____

_____

_____

_____

_____

_____

_____

_____

KEY TAKEAWAYS

- Begin by developing a clear picture of what your ideal life looks like.
- Reflect back to your childhood for things that brought you fun and joy.
- Focus on doing what you LOVE to do.
- Aim to do things that energize you rather than drain you.
- Don't forget to play!

Step Three

Become Aware

> *You cannot heal what you do not know.*
> —Author Unknown

Many of us are not even aware of the real rocks in our buckets that are preventing us from moving from our current situation to our ideal life. We may know what would make us happier, but we feel stuck. I firmly believe that it is the unaddressed rocks in our buckets that keep us from moving forward toward our happier selves. Unless we know what the rocks are, we can't address them.

When we are born, our brains are a clean, blank slate much like a computer hard drive or flash drive with nothing recorded on it. Yes, we are all products of hereditary traits, factors that may have affected us while in the womb, and environmental events. For the purpose of this book, I am referring to the environmental influences. We don't arrive in this world with any preconceived ideas that we are good or bad, enough or not enough, wanted or not wanted.

However, as soon as we are born, we start receiving messages, some positive and some negative. The good messages help us have confidence and pride. Telling a child they are smart, talented, loved, appreciated, athletic, or pretty/handsome leads to positive self-talk.

Children also hear negative messages such as:

- "You're doing it wrong."
- "You spilled your drink again!"
- "How can you be so clumsy?"
- "Why are you so whiny all the time?"

Toss the Rocks and Get on With It!

- "How can you be so stupid?"
- "Be quiet. You talk too much."

When we receive negative messages, they are captured as data on our "hard drive." Because we are children, we assume these negative messages are true. Often we go through life internalizing and believing these negative characteristics, thus limiting our potential in life. People react differently and while these comments may not affect some, for others it can lead to low self-esteem, lack of confidence and negative self-talk.

When my daughter was around five years old, we were at a friend's house and she and Lucy were playing "bat the ball." Lucy hit the ball and her parents said, "Lucy, you can do better than that! That was awful." My daughter hit the ball and regardless of how bad it was, we said, "Great try, Katie. Hit it again!" Who do you think grew up with more confidence? Lucy became afraid to try things and when someone laughed when she did something cute or funny, she would hide behind her parents because she felt people were laughing AT her. I certainly did not do everything right... far from it, but I am very aware of the impact of words on a child.

Let's put something on the table. We will talk a good deal about parents in this book because of the dramatic impact parents have on their children's lives. However, I am in no way blaming parents. I truly believe, that in almost all cases, parents are doing what they think is best for their children. I believe parents do not intend harm, but nevertheless, unintended hurts can happen.

I read the following several years ago, and it rings so true:

> "One of the paradoxes of life is that, though most of us suffered varying degrees of childhood pain, few know how to spare their own children."[1]

---

[1] Overeaters Anonymous, *For Today* (New Mexico: Overeaters Anonymous, Inc., 1982), 215.

I have come to realize that parents cannot give what they don't have. If they were not shown love, for example, they may have a hard time expressing it. If a person grows up in an abusive family full of chaos, they may tend to create chaos because that's what they know.

Experiences also occur that can negatively impact us and record damaging data on our hard drives. I vividly remember being 8 years old, and a classmate shouted, "Look at Donna. She is wearing boy's shoes." I wanted to sink into the sidewalk. I was born with a club foot and wore orthopedic shoes, as well as having casts on for the first 7 years of my life. I already felt "different," and that peer comment made me feel even more self-conscious. It was so vivid that I still remember his name and where I was standing.

As we become adults, more is recorded as we experience careers, marriage, children, and various relationships. If any of these causes a negative rock to fly into your bucket, you will need to decide if you want to carry it around for the rest of your life or toss the rock!

Be mindful that both good and bad messages get recorded, but most of us tend to focus on the negative. For example, think of the last time you received an annual appraisal or review. Let's say you were told a number of good things that you have been doing, and you were also told that you could improve your interpersonal skills with your peers. You come home and tell your spouse or significant other. The conversation may go something like this, "My manager had the NERVE to tell me that I stink at dealing with my peers. How dare he!" And the good comments were lost! Does this ring a bell?

Before I have you dive into becoming aware of your own rocks, it's important to understand the difference between a symptom and a cause. For example, a headache is a <u>symptom.</u> The underlying <u>cause</u> could be anything from poor eyesight, allergies, stress, a brain tumor, or something else. We must figure out the cause, in order to heal the headache.

Let's look at Barry's story. Barry had been abusing alcohol for years. The alcohol abuse was the <u>symptom.</u> The underlying <u>cause</u> was that Barry was self-medicating to escape from his emotional pain. Barry was very stressed from work. Although he was doing a good job, there were layoffs several times a year. Barry had a wife who didn't work and two young children. He lived in fear that he could be next on the chopping block. He ramped up his work hours which had the adverse effect of putting stress on his relationship with his wife and children. He often would miss dinner with the family or his children's sports games. He couldn't see a way out, so he drank and numbed the pain. His biggest pain was fear, the real "rock in his bucket." Once he began to address his fears, life got better. Barry did not get laid off, but he did develop a back-up plan for what he would do if he lost his job. This brought him some peace and reduced his stress.

As a final example, I will use myself. You already know about my fear of getting married. My freshman year in college, I met the "boy of my dreams." We dated throughout college with plans to get married when we graduated. Then the time came, and I froze. Although I desperately wanted to spend my life with this man, I would have nightmares that it was my wedding day, and I could not go down the aisle. He finally gave up and left me, and I was devastated. I had no idea as to my "WHY." I knew I had a fear of marriage, but it took me years to figure out the root cause and address the fear. It had nothing to do with my boyfriend. It had everything to do with me! The years of hearing "Don't ever get married, don't ever have kids, it will ruin your life" had taken a toll on me. I eventually did address this fear, and I'm glad I did; otherwise, I would not have the life of joy that I have today.

YOUR TURN!

Reflection Time

It is important to make this YOUR story. You need to be aware of what your rocks are. Following are several self-assessments to help you discover the rocks that are holding you back from experiencing genuine joy in your life. Please take the time to invest in yourself. I know this may be hard but dig deep and be brutally honest.

REFLECTION EXERCISE

1. Name any negative *words* about yourself that you heard or felt during childhood.

_____

_____

_____

_____

_____

_____

_____

2. Name any negative *experiences* that had an impact on you during your childhood.

_____

_____

_____

_____

_____

_____

_____

3. How do the above past experiences impact your life today?

_____
_____
_____
_____
_____
_____
_____

LIFE STORY LOOK-BACK EXERCISE

Now, let's take a deeper dive. This exercise takes you further into understanding how your past may be affecting your present and future. The top horizontal row represents your life from birth to the present. The bottom row represents low points in your life. List your top five low points along with your corresponding age in each of the five columns. The purpose is to uncover rocks that you are unaware of, and to bring known ones to light.

To give you an idea, below are several examples:

KEN'S LOOK-BACK

Birth - age 7	age 8	age 10	age 16	age 35
Emotional neglect	Bullied	Parents' divorce	Didn't make the football team	Laid off from job

Some of Ken's rocks include lack of self-confidence, anger, fear of loss, financial insecurity, and doubt. You can see from his Life Look-Back where these came from!

And to be honest and transparent, here is my look-back:

DONNA'S LOOK-BACK

Ages 1-38	age 8	age 21	age 22	age 22-52
Hearing Mantra*	OCD onset	Broken relationship	Not getting job of my dreams	Career that was not my passion
*Don't ever get married, don't ever have kids. It will ruin your life.					

Some of my rocks accordingly were fears of marriage, having children, being rejected again, feeling not good enough, insecurity, and fear of making mistakes.

YOUR TURN!

AGE:					
LOW POINT:					

Once you are finished, go back, and ask yourself if you left anything out. I did a similar exercise with a group and during the debrief, we each shared our stories. Andy shared the low points he had written down. Later, he mentioned that he and his siblings had been abandoned by their dad when he was around six years old. He had buried this pain and was just then realizing the impact it had on him!

Another friend of mine had been sexually abused as a child by her grandfather and had completely repressed it. As an adult, she kept feeling that something was missing. Through therapy in her 50s, the memories came flooding back. Only then was she able to process it, forgive, and free herself from the rocks in her bucket caused by this trauma.

If anybody got teary eyed thinking about an event, it's because it still stings and is a BIG rock. I do NOT want you to get stuck in your past. You are NOT your past. Nobody can trap you in your past except yourself. You can choose to be free and live your life differently. Don't let anything from your past steal your joy!!

If you do not process your past, your past can determine your present and future.
—Donna Strong

YOUR TURN: NAME YOUR ROCKS

Now it's your turn to make a list of the rocks in your own bucket. Use your answers from the first reflection section in this chapter, along with your Life Story Look-Back to uncover the rocks you are carrying. List below as many of your rocks as you can think of. Be brutally honest. Dig deep. You are the only one who needs to see this unless you choose to share. Don't try to be perfect. You can keep adding to this list during your journey.

ROCKS IN (write your name here) Bucket:

1.

2.

3.

4.

5.

6.

7.

8.

9.

10.

Congratulations! You just completed a hard exercise that many people do not even think about. Just remember, you do not have to live this way. You are powerful and capable of tossing these rocks and moving to a happier life full of joy, happiness, and purpose.

Whatever you have done or experienced in your past does not define you. You can have a different and brighter future. Your past does not have to be your future. You are free to choose a different life.

KEY TAKEAWAYS

- You must dig deep and become AWARE of your rocks in order to implement positive change.
- If you do not PROCESS your past, it can negatively impact your present and future.
- You are NOT your past.

Step Four
Count the Cost

> *Getting over a painful experience is much like crossing monkey bars.*
> *You have to let go at some point in order to move forward.*
> — *C.S. Lewis*

There is a cost associated with carrying around our bucket of rocks. Our buckets hold all kinds of unresolved experiences and beliefs that impact our ability to live our best lives. If we allow our buckets to fill up, and never toss out any of the rocks, it can bring us to our knees. You do not need to carry all that weight! You can decide to toss these rocks!

To do this, it helps to look at what it is costing you to carry all these rocks, pebbles, and boulders in your bucket. In this chapter, you will look at what each of YOUR rocks are costing you and decide if you are willing to toss them.

You will ask yourself, for each rock, "WHAT IS IT COSTING ME?" For example:

- Does your mind continue to spin about this issue?
- Do you have tightness in your shoulders and neck?
- Are you having upset stomachs or headaches?
- Is it impacting your current relationships?
- Do they interfere with your professional goals? Health? Enjoyment of life?

Our rocks can drain us of energy, impact our relationships, and steal our joy. Suppose your bucket contained one rock of insecurity, three rocks of resentment, one boulder of mistrust, and three rocks of fear. How would it feel to carry this bucket?

The problem is that often we have accumulated our rocks slowly over time, and we are not aware of the increasing weight. Perhaps we have tried to look at them but deemed it too difficult or painful. Instead, we just threw some dirt on the rocks to cover them up, and we went on down the road of life carrying this unwieldy bucket. Or perhaps we started blaming others for our rocks when the real problem is us. Maybe we have neglected to address the rocks, look at our part of the problem and make changes.

Letting our rocks pile up over time is like the "frog in the boiling water" story. It is a metaphor used to illustrate how people may fail to notice gradual changes, leading to adverse outcomes. There are various versions, but here is mine:

There was a frog happily living in the pond, enjoying the beautiful surroundings, the comfortable weather, and blue sky. It saw a pot of water nearby and hopped over to check it out. The frog did not realize that a fire had been built under the pot. Out of curiosity, it hopped into the pot. The frog was unaware that the temperature was slowly getting hotter. It continued to swim around until it became unbearably hot. But it was too late as the boiling water had overcome him.

A cold frog was hopping along near the pot and saw the frog in distress. He hopped into the pot, and immediately hopped out, pulling the first frog out with him, saving them both from impending death.

Metaphorically, the frog story is often used to emphasize the dangers of complacency and the need to be aware of gradual changes in our lives so that we can take proactive action before it is too late.

Tying this back to rocks in our bucket, the point is that if we are not careful, we could be sitting in a pot of hot water and not realize what it is costing us. Therein lies the necessity to take off the blinders and address the negative aspects that are keeping us from enjoying our best lives!

I will sometimes invite Melissa, my good friend and confidante, to jump into my bucket. Something might be troubling me, and I just can't figure it out by myself. She will figuratively jump into my bucket and point out things I am either not aware of, or I am avoiding! This helps me see what it is costing me to continue to carry my rocks vs tossing them out, one by one.

My coaching clients are typically aware of their rocks on some level. My role is to shine a light on the rocks and encourage them to make any changes that will improve their lives.

Let's look at a few examples:

BEN'S STORY OF BULLYING

As a child, Ben was bullied by his peers. The boys put him down because he was uncoordinated and did poorly in sports. Nobody wanted Ben on their team. They called him names and degraded him. Ben did not speak up and tell anyone. Sadly, this is often the case.

The bullying continued in middle school and high school. He began to feel like a freak and lost his self-confidence and pride. Over time, his anxiety and depression turned to anger. He hated the boys who had bullied him, and he constantly revisited these episodes as an adult.

So, what is it costing Ben? These long-lost acquaintances are no longer thinking about Ben. But Ben is thinking about them! It's as if they are "renting space" in Ben's head! The impact is that Ben has a hard time making friends and building relationships due to a lack of trust. He has never tossed the rocks and gained the confidence to move forward. He feels lonely and says that every day is a challenge.

I wish all stories had a good outcome, but in Ben's case this is not true…yet!

Only Ben can make the changes. He is the only one that can ensure he "gets out of the boiling pot of water." For each of you, it's a choice that only you can make.

Below are some generalized stories about people carrying around emotional rocks and what it is costing them:

1. Fear of Failure
- Story: Rick had a bad experience in his career and developed a fear of failure.
- Cost: Rick avoided taking on new assignments or challenges, limiting his promotions, overall career growth and his earning power.

2. Unresolved Childhood Trauma
- Story: Gene experienced childhood trauma that he never addressed. He buried these memories deep within his bucket and threw dirt over the rocks so that he could escape from the memories.
- Cost: Gene's unresolved trauma led to anxiety and depression, affecting his emotional well-being and ability to form relationships.

3. Perfectionism
- Story: Peggy learned early in life that perfectionism helped her prevent mistakes and excel in her activities. She took this perfectionism too far and it became an obsession.
- Cost: Peggy's perfectionism led to slowness, anxiety, and relationship issues.

4. Unforgiven Resentment
- Story: Rose held onto a grudge from her broken marriage. She could not forgive and move on, and she refused to see

her part. She played the role of victim and constantly talked about it around her friends.
- Cost: Rose avoided getting into new relationships due to a lack of trust, hindering her ability to find happiness. Some of her friends distanced themselves from her, due to her continual complaining. This led to sadness and loneliness.

5. Regret from Unfulfilled Passion
- Story: Leah regretted not pursuing her passion for working in the airline industry. Due to family expectations, she took a job that paid well but did not excite her. She regretted this throughout her life.
- Cost: Leah experienced a sense of unfulfillment and struggled with a job that was not really in her wheelhouse. This impacted her job satisfaction, happiness, and joy.

6. Family Secret Revealed
- Story: Emma discovered, after the death of her parents, that she was adopted!
- Cost: Emma's discovery led to questions, disbelief, and feelings of betrayal because she had not been told by her parents. It caused Emma to struggle with a sense of belonging, and subsequently led to a great deal of anger.

YOUR TURN!

Now it's YOUR turn to answer the question of "What is it costing me?" Go back to the end of Step 3 where you listed your rocks. Copy your rocks into the left column of the table below and complete columns 2 and 3 for each rock.

ROCKS IN MY BUCKET	WHAT IS IT COSTING ME?	AM I WILLING TO CHANGE?

Are you ready and willing to toss the rocks? It takes courage, but if you do not toss the rocks, what will your life look like in five years? If you are ready, let's go! The next section of the book will give you strategies on HOW to toss your rocks and move to your ideal life of joy.

KEY TAKEAWAYS

- There is a cost to hanging on to your rocks.
- Sitting in the "pot of boiling water" too long can be painful in the end.
- You are the only one who can make the decision to change.

PART 2

Get Rid of the Rocks Already!

In this section, we cover Step Five: Toss the Rocks. Each chapter will look at one of the six most common rocks, along with strategies for HOW to toss these rocks. You have done the hard part of becoming aware of your rocks and looking at what it is costing you to hang on to them.

We'll now take a deep dive into the following six common rocks:

- Fear
- Insecurity and Self-Doubt
- Perfectionism
- People-pleasing
- Resentments
- Addictions

You may be wondering why "anger" is not included. It is because anger is a disguise; it is a mask for pain. Anger is not the primary emotion. The primary emotion is what is underneath the anger. Asking a person WHY they are angry will lead you to the primary emotion. The primary emotion underneath the anger is the "rock" that is causing the pain. Anger could be a mask for fear, frustration, shame, jealousy, self-doubt, resentments, or other hurts. Addressing these rocks can calm the anger.

Are you ready to look at ways to toss those rocks? Let's go!

Step Five
Toss the Rocks

Rock #1: Lose the Fear

> "Too many of us are not living our dreams because we are living our fears."
> —Les Brown

The above quote speaks volumes! Some of you may be so controlled by fear that you make decisions based on fear or stay "stuck" in a situation where you are not happy. In this chapter, we will address the HOW of breaking the chains that keep you in bondage...those fears that prevent you from realizing your dreams.

For me, fear was the biggest rock in my bucket. Actually, it was a boulder and for many years, kept me from living the life I wanted to live. My fears ranged from the fear of speaking up in case I was wrong and would look stupid, fear of making changes because I might pick the wrong path, fear of marriage and having a child because I was told early on that would ruin my life, fear of being hurt again, fear of switching companies even though I knew the industry that excited me, fear of making mistakes...and the list goes on.

Typically, we live alone with our fears. We are afraid to express them out of shame, fear of appearing weak, or simply because it scares us to face our fears. The irony is that keeping our secrets to ourselves is detrimental to our ability to overcome these fears and move forward with courage.

Some fears are rational such as the fear we experience when we see a rattlesnake or bear, or the fear of seeing a truck coming straight at you at 100 mph. These are warranted fears that prevent us from harm.

However, other types of fears are irrational. Instead of helping us, these irrational fears hurt us and prevent us from pursuing what is important to us. Many of these fears are created in our own minds. Or someone else puts these fears in our minds, even though they simply are not true. Fear tells us that we are not good enough, not loved, not worthy, not smart enough, that we will never succeed, or that we don't have what it takes. These are all lies. We all have far more capacity and capabilities than we give ourselves credit for.

As adults, we may have a fear that seems strange, but we aren't in touch with where the fear comes from. In the book *What Happened to You?* by Oprah Winfrey and Bruce D. Perry, M.D., Ph.D. Oprah talks about her fear of being alone at night. She said her fear did not make sense and that it kept getting worse. Later in life, a long-forgotten memory emerged that helped her understand the origin of this fear.[1]

Oprah spent her early childhood living with her grandmother, Hattie Mae. She always slept with her grandmother, while her grandfather, who had dementia, slept in another room. One night Oprah was suddenly awakened. Her grandfather had come into their bedroom and was trying to strangle her grandmother. Hattie Mae managed to push her husband off her and she ran out of the house to get help from a neighbor to put him back in his bedroom.

After this episode, Oprah's grandmother always slept with a chair wedged under the doorknob of her bedroom door. She also hung tin cans on the door to warn her if someone tried to enter. This instilled a fear in Oprah, causing her to sleep "on alert" at night, making sure the tin cans did not rattle.

---

1 Bruce D. Perry, M.D., Ph.D. and Oprah Winfrey, *What Happened to You? Conversations on Trauma, Resilience, and Healing* (New York: Flatiron Books, 2021), 17, 123–124,

As an adult, Oprah finally connected the dots and realized that she had carried this childhood fear into her adult life! She had suppressed this traumatizing event for years, but it finally re-emerged and brought her clarity. Once she discovered the "why," she was able to step back whenever the fear resurfaced, and choose to move through the fear.

In their book, Oprah and Dr. Bruce Perry pose a very different question. Instead of asking "What's wrong with you," they recommend asking, "What happened to you?" They point out that this shift in perspective recognizes the power of the past to shape our current way of functioning.

This indeed is precisely the question we should be asking. We have been conditioned to think and feel a certain way by our environmental influences. This conditioning has resulted in many of the "rocks" we are carrying in our buckets. It is not your fault! There is nothing wrong with you!

Just as Oprah had fear as a "rock in her bucket," so do most of us. The reason is that fear encompasses so many categories, such as the fear of:

- Failure
- Change
- Being judged
- Inadequacy
- Rejection
- Criticism
- Loss of love
- Public speaking
- Health issues
- Commitment
- The future
- The unknown

- Getting old
- Death
- Something bad happening
- Not having enough money

You can probably think of other fears too. The list is endless!

YOUR TURN!

What are your fears? Write them down below.

1.

2.

3.

4.

5.

6.

Think about what it is costing you to hold on to these fears. Think about the cost you experience from not taking on new opportunities and adventures.

When you give in to fear, you are limiting yourself. I have a sorority sister who has a terrible fear of flying. However, she did not want to miss out on college homecoming weekends, annual sorority reunions, or trips with her family and friends. She realized that her fear of flying was limiting her opportunities and making her world too small. She decided to overcome her fear by getting on the plane and doing it anyhow. It still gives her anxiety even thinking about an upcoming trip, but it no longer paralyzes her nor prevents her from traveling.

It's as if fear puts us in a box. If we stay there, we feel safe. But the cost of staying in our "box" can be tragic. As we discussed earlier, it's better to get to the end of your life and say, "I had a great ride" rather than to say, "I wish I would have."

Last summer my husband, daughter, and I were sitting in a circle on our beach chairs at Amelia Island. It was a beautiful day, and the sound of the ocean was soothing. I realized that if I had not overcome my fears, that gift of family would never have happened. Those two incredible human beings would not have been a part of my life. I thank God every day for His intervention and for giving me strength and courage to get beyond my fears.

So how do we deal with fear?
First, we must each CHOOSE not to let our fears control us. We need to FACE the rocks in our bucket instead of letting them dominate us.

Seven Strategies for Losing the Fear

1. Become aware of your fears. Acknowledge them and name them.

    Some of our fears may be subtle and you don't even realize they are controlling your life. You must dig deep to see them. Once brought to light, you can view them from a rational perspective and often conclude that the fear is unwarranted.

2. Talk about your fears to someone you trust.

   Often people hide their fears and are afraid to discuss them with anybody. I firmly believe that "secrets make us sick." Left to our own devices, our fear can become overwhelming. By telling your "secret" to someone you trust, it often loses its power. Plus, you then have someone who can see your fears via a different lens and can help and support you.

3. Remind yourself what fear is costing you.

   What are you missing out on because you are allowing the fear to control you? Bringing this "lost opportunity" cost to the forefront of your consciousness can give you the critical push to act. Odds are your fears are not only affecting you, but also your family and friends. For example, if you have a fear of speaking in public, it will affect your opportunity to make a bigger impact. If you fear taking on a more responsible job with better pay, you are affecting your family's financial picture as well. Get honest with yourself and don't let your fears impact you, your family, your friends, or your business.

4. Look at the evidence.

   Do research to see if your fear is logical and rational. Is your fear factual? The acronym F.E.A.R. stands for "False Evidence Appearing Real." Sometimes just realizing how irrational the fear is will help move you past the fear.

5. Surrender.

> Are you sick and tired of living in fear? You always have the choice to surrender. You can make up your mind that you absolutely will no longer let fear dictate your life. Turn it over to God.... surrender the fear!
>
> At age thirty-five, I was sick and tired of my fear of getting married. I was tired of being alone. I realized that, unless I gained courage, I would end up old and by myself. It was then that I opened myself up to God and asked him to bring the right man into my life. It was a beautiful Sunday afternoon, and I was on an airplane bound for Phoenix to visit a girlfriend. I had just ended a four-year relationship with the wrong man. You see, I also had a fear of ending things (to me it was like quitting, and I thought that was a form of failure).
>
> I was hoping that nobody would sit beside me because I was working on a project. Something inspired me to pray, "Dear God, I give up on men and relationships. If you want me to meet someone, you must bring him right here to me and put him clearly in front of me." Just then, the flight attendant announced that the plane door had been closed and we were ready for take-off. A few minutes later, an announcement was made that the door was being opened to allow a passenger on board. We all know that would never happen today!
>
> A man walked down the aisle, and I again prayed—this time that the man did not sit beside me. You see, I was busy! Well, he took the seat right next to me. We talked the entire way to Dallas, where we were each making a connecting flight. He was not the "stereotypical" man I usually dated. In hindsight, I realize that God gives us what we need, not necessarily what we think we want. This man became my

husband, and we recently celebrated thirty-one wonderful years of marriage.

This would never have happened if I had not surrendered and opened myself up to facing my fear and walking through it instead of running back to safety.

6. Walk THROUGH the fear, not under or around it.

Even though you are afraid of something, decide to do it anyhow! Afraid of flying? Get on the plane! Afraid of public speaking? Get on the stage! Do it again and again. As you walk *through* the fear, the fear will start to subside. You will get more comfortable and gain confidence. You will get to the other side of fear. Don't wait until you are no longer scared. That day may never come.

Keep in mind that fear is like a wave. A wave begins to form and gets bigger and bigger until it reaches a crest, and then it crashes and subsides. When we approach a fear, we have anxiety that gains momentum and builds much like a wave. The closer we get to walking through the fear, the more intense the fear and emotions become. Once they peak, the anxiety diminishes.

Be willing to take risks. It's the way you learn and grow. Albert Einstein was quoted as saying:

A ship is always safe at the shore, but that is not what it is built for.

7. If you are unable to conquer the fear, seek help.

This is not a weakness, but a brave step of how determined you are to set yourself free. One of the best therapies for addressing fear is Cognitive Behavioral Therapy (CBT).

One part of CBT treatment that is often used for fears is Exposure Treatment. This therapy involves gradually confronting the source of the fear in order to break the cycle of avoidance.

For example, when I went through Exposure Treatment for my OCD, one of the fears I had was germs. I had been taught that dogs are dirty and that if you pet an animal, you needed to wash your hands before touching anything in the house. My childhood dog was an outdoor dog, so I was constantly having to wash my hands whenever I entered the house, especially before I touched food. My therapist had me start petting the dog that was in her office. I would have to go all day without washing my hands. I even had to fix food and eat it! Anxiety! With exposure, my fear subsided. In my adult life, I have had dogs that were my babies. They slept in our bed, ate out of my hand, and camped out on our furniture. The fear was gone!

This process works well with all kinds of fears. It is extremely effective and powerful. If you choose this path, you will gain incredible freedom in knowing your fear no longer has power over you.

Fears can be scary, stubborn, and frustrating. Don't let your gremlin tell you that you can't do something. You can! Don't let your fears keep you from reaching your true happiness and joy! And don't procrastinate—take action now!

Rock #2: Drop the Insecurity and Self-Doubt

Doubt kills more dreams than failure ever will.
—*Suzy Kassem*

I was leading a class in Dallas, Texas, back in my early thirties. A girl came up to me after the class and told me I should make audio training tapes because I was such a good instructor.

I replied, "That will never fly. I have a southern accent, and people think southerners are slow and/or stupid."

She said, "That's not true. My favorite audio tape series is by a female from Texas who has a very thick accent. I will give you a set of her audios and you can listen for yourself."

Then a good friend walked into the classroom and watched me while she was waiting for our lunch break. At lunch, she looked at me in surprise and said "You are very good at speaking. You should do something with that."

What do you think I did? I did nothing! Why? Because my internal self-talk told me a different story. It told me that I didn't have the correct accent to be a success and I wasn't good enough to create something on my own. Although I was an instructor for IBM for many years, and held hundreds of workshops, I never felt that I was great. I lacked the self-confidence to take the leap to explore my abilities and opportunities.

Does this sound familiar? Everybody has insecurities. We may look at someone who appears to have it all — looks, money, a prestigious career, the "perfect" family—and we may wonder why that can't be us. The reality is that at some level, every person has their own set of insecurities and struggles. You see this with celebrities who look so perfect and then we hear they are getting a divorce or have addiction issues.

Rock #2: Drop the Insecurity and Self-Doubt

Think about Marilyn Monroe, who struggled with insecurity and self-esteem despite her fame and glory as a sex symbol and actress. Even Abraham Lincoln, one of our greatest presidents, suffered from depression and insecurity.

This demonstrates that insecurities can affect any of us, regardless of fame and success. If you too suffer from insecurities, you are not alone. The important part is to do the work to change your situation.

We are not born with insecurities and self-doubt. They are learned messages based on things that have been said to us, or things we have experienced in life. People may have said discouraging things to us such as:

- You're too old.
- You're too young and inexperienced.
- That will never work.
- You're not smart enough.
- It's too risky.
- You'll never make any money doing that.
- No one cares about that.
- That field is already saturated.

Or we may lack security based on past experiences such as:

- Being bullied and told we were no good.
- Failing to make the baseball and the basketball teams.
- Girls giggling at us because we were fat.
- Being passed up for a promotion we felt we deserved.
- Experiencing abuse as a child and feeling it must be our fault.

Any of these comments and experiences can cause us to feel insecure IF we allow it. At some point, we must STOP this downward and useless spiral, and CHOOSE to turn it around. When your bucket gets too heavy and you become frustrated, tired, depressed or angry, you know it's time to make a change. You have the power to do this... all you have to do is choose it, claim it and take action. I am not saying it is easy, but it is so worth it. And remember, your past does not define you!

When you doubt yourself, you feel insecure. It's important to break this cycle in order to reach your full potential and experience a joyful life.

Like all the rocks in our bucket, we gather these along our life's journey. The bucket gets heavy, and it is our responsibility and choice to toss the rocks.

Let's explore our insecurities and self-doubt and look at HOW to overcome negative, internal self-talk so we can be the best possible version of ourselves. My goal is that you will spring free of doubt and insecurities and lean into what you really want to do and are designed to do!

Seven Strategies for Dropping the Insecurity and Self-Doubt

1. Acknowledge your insecurities.

We must first know what insecurities are tripping us up. Ask yourself if you are insecure about any of the following:

- Relationships
- Professional/career life
- What other people think about you
- Making a decision
- Social situations
- Physical appearance
- Finances
- Intellectual abilities
- Not speaking up for fear of looking stupid
- Shying away from something when deep down you want to participate

YOUR TURN!

Write down your Top 5 insecurities below:

1.

2.

3.

4.

5.

This first step of acknowledging your insecurities allows you to own them and know what you need to work on.

2. Identify your negative self-talk and replace it with positive self-talk.

Our self-talk is so powerful. If we continually tell ourselves negative things, we can come to believe it! Sometimes negative self-talk becomes a habit, and we are not even aware that we are our own worst enemy.

You CAN change your self-talk. It takes effort and persistence, but it works. When you realize that you are participating in negative self-talk, pause and ask yourself, "How can I think about this differently?" Create a positive message to tell yourself instead of allowing your mood to spiral downward by the negativity.

Here are some examples of how it works:

YOUR NEGATIVE INNER VOICE	YOUR POSITIVE INNER VOICE
I keep making mistakes. What is wrong with me?	Everybody makes mistakes. I will learn from my mistakes and improve.
I'm not smart enough to do this job.	I am intelligent and have talents and strengths that will help me be successful.
I am such a failure. Look what a mess I made of things.	This is just one instance. I will learn from it and be successful in the future. I am resilient and determined.
I will never get this project completed. I am so slow!	Look at the progress I have already made. I will keep moving forward, one day at a time, and complete the project on time.
I'll never be good enough.	I am good enough just as I am. I will continue to improve and work on things I deem important. I am capable and deserve to be happy.

YOUR TURN!

Take some time to practice this powerful tool now. List some of your negative self-talk and what you can say positively to yourself instead:

YOUR NEGATIVE INNER VOICE	YOUR POSITIVE INNER VOICE

Rock #2: Drop the Insecurity and Self-Doubt

Practice this method daily until positive self-talk becomes your new normal. If you slide back, just pause, and reframe your thinking. I truly believe that if you change your thoughts, you can change your life!

3. Challenge negative thoughts.

With this technique, I want you to argue with yourself. When a negative thought pops into your head, such as, "I can't do anything right," ask yourself questions such as:

- Is that really true?
- Where did that message come from?
- Why should I believe it?
- Are my insecurities based on fact?

Sometimes we fall into all-or-nothing thinking. We think that just because we can't do this one thing, we can't do anything. Or we may fall into the trap of projection, thinking that because we can't do something now, we will NEVER be able to do it. All of this is false thinking. It is all negative. Challenge these thoughts and see where it takes you!

4. Focus on your strengths.

Everyone comes to the table with their own set of natural talents and strengths. These are our innate abilities. Often, they come so easily to us that we assume everyone has them. They don't! Our talents are like a thumbprint, unique only to us.

People often cannot identify their strengths but are quick to name their weaknesses. Focusing on your weaknesses reinforces your feelings of insecurity and self-doubt, and is counter-productive.

Instead, do a mind shift. Focus on your strengths, not your weaknesses.

First, think about and then WRITE down your natural talents. In order to identify these, ask yourself these questions:

What activities am I:

- Naturally drawn to?
- Able to pick up quickly?
- Looking forward to doing again?
- Completing faster than other people?
- Able to do naturally and easily?

These are your natural talents, and to the degree you can stay in your lane in your business and personal life, you will feel much more secure about your abilities and self-worth.

Your Turn: Top 5 Strengths

Think of the Top 5 things you like about yourself and know you are good at doing. These can be things such as: I am smart, I am fun to be around, I am caring, I am responsible, I love thinking strategically and figuring out a plan, I'm a great problem-solver, I build relationships easily, I'm a great organizer, or a natural leader.

Write your 5 strengths below:

1.

2.

3.

4.

5.

Now take this list and go to a mirror. Look yourself in the mirror and tell yourself these five things every day for the next 21 days. You may feel awkward at first, but do it anyhow. It will make a difference in your self-image and your sense of security.

Remember that you have a wonderful, unique set of talents. Stay in your strength zone as much as possible. Ask for assignments that take advantage of your strengths. You will feel more confident using this method, and your insecurity and doubt will decrease. Nobody can be good at everything, so don't try. Just remember to "stay in your lane."

5. Use positive affirmations.

Positive affirmations are positive statements that are to be repeated on a regular basis with the intention of building a positive mindset and self-confidence. Affirmations help overcome negative or self-sabotaging thoughts, replacing them with empowering and uplifting beliefs.

Repetition is very important. By repeating affirmations often, the brain begins to take these positive affirmations as facts. The subconscious mind is influenced by what the conscious mind tells it. Over time, with repetition and consistency, these positive affirmations can begin to change your subconscious beliefs and perceptions, leading to positive changes.

A good time to repeat your list of affirmations is the first thing in the morning. This helps you meet challenges with a stronger and more optimistic outlook during the day. I also find it helpful to repeat an affirmation whenever a negative thought pops into my head during the day. For example, if self-doubt creeps in, I like to tell myself, "I am confident and capable…. I am confident and capable…I am confident and capable." The repetition drowns out the negative thought and propels me to keep moving forward.

When creating your own affirmation list, it is beneficial to keep them short, concise, and specific. They must be positive and in the PRESENT tense. Do not use words such as "try," "attempt," or "hope." Your affirmation is affirming that what you want to become the truth already is the truth.

To get you started, here are some examples of affirmations:

1. I am confident in my abilities.

2. I have strengths that are powerful.

3. I am beautiful/handsome both inside and out.

4. I am enough just as I am.

5. I choose happiness and joy every day.

6. I attract positive and loving relationships into my life.

7. I am surrounded by supportive people.

8. I am worthy of self-care and nurturing.

9. I trust my intuition and know that the Holy Spirit guides me.

10. I attract opportunity, abundance, and prosperity into my life.

11. I nourish my body with healthy food and exercise.

12. I am loved.
13. I am a good person.
14. I am a caring person.
15. I respect myself.
16. I prioritize my rest and peace of mind.
17. I am a good presenter.
18. I am optimistic.
19. I am resilient.
20. I have a purpose that brings me joy.

YOUR TURN!

Make a list of affirmations that fit your personal situation. Feel free to use the ones above or create new ones that align with your personal goals and values. Remember to phrase your affirmations in the present tense, as if they are already true. Start with your "top 10" and later you can expand on them.

1.

2.

3.

4.

5.

6.

7.

8.

9.

10.

Remember to repeat these regularly – in the morning, before bed, or anytime throughout the day when you need a positivity boost. Many people find it helpful to post their affirmations on their mirror.

6. Replace "what if" with "so what."

This is one of the best pieces of advice I ever received! It's so simple, yet so powerful. Although it is really part of positive self-talk, I wanted to call it out as a separate technique because it is so helpful.

For years, I was constantly telling myself, "But what if this happens?" or "What if that happens?" I was looking at the negative, at the glass half empty. "What if" was my standard question to myself and prevented me from taking on challenges and new opportunities. It kept me from growing.

When someone told me to replace my "What if?" with "So what?" I was stunned. I had never thought about it. It took me time to get used to this concept. This approach opens doors to opportunity and growth.

The conversation goes like this:

Mary: WHAT IF I change classes and I hate the new one?
Comeback: SO WHAT? It is only for one semester, not forever!

Bill: WHAT IF I take this new job and I don't like the people?

Rock #2: Drop the Insecurity and Self-Doubt

SO WHAT? I can learn to get along with anyone. If the environment gets too toxic, I will look for another job.

Jane: WHAT IF I am too old to start a new career?
SO WHAT? If I don't try, I will always regret it. I feel qualified and passionate about this new endeavor.

It's about opening doors versus shutting them.

7. Surround yourself with people who support you.

Surround yourself with people who accept you as you are. Choose to be around those who support what you are trying to accomplish. These are your cheerleaders and will keep you moving toward your goals and desires. Spending time with them will increase your confidence and reduce your insecurities.

In a work environment, this is not always possible. We are put on teams with a mix of people, some who we may not like or work well with. My advice is to do your best. You don't have to be their best friend or even like them. You just have to get the work accomplished. If you keep an open mind, and look for the good in the other person, you may end up liking them. This happened to me with an arrogant and demanding second-line manager. Once I got to know him as a person, my opinion shifted drastically, and we became friends.

A friend or spouse may be your negative source. It is your responsibility to tell them the impact their comments have on you. Remember, you do not have the power to change the other person. Just surround yourself with positive affirmations and self-talk, and touch base with your support group often.

In summary, you have the power within you to retrain your mind to focus on your positive attributes and natural strengths instead of your perceived weaknesses. This reduces your self-doubt and insecurity. Some insecurities may always be there, and this is natural. The important thing is that you have the ability to dial down the volume. Just keep putting one foot in front of the other. We are all works in progress.

Rock #3: Free Yourself of Perfectionism

Perfectionism is a self-destructive and addictive belief system that fuels this primary thought: If I look perfect, and do everything perfectly, I can avoid or minimize the painful feelings of shame, judgment, and blame.
—*Brené Brown*[1]

Perfectionism can be crippling. There is a difference between doing your best and trying to be perfect. For those of us who suffer from perfectionism, you know how frustrating and time-consuming it can be. We are not sure what drives us, but we feel we must get it right or something bad could happen. Perhaps it's a feeling of insecurity and we think we might look stupid if we make mistakes. Perhaps it's a fear that if we're not perfect, we might not get that promotion or we might get laid off. Whatever the reason, we are irrationally trying to protect ourselves from hurt.

It's irrational because no human is perfect. We're striving for something that is unattainable. Our expectations are far exceeding normal abilities. At some point we realize the cost is too high. It is slowing us down and we can't keep up. In that moment, we determine we must do something about it. If this resonates with you, keep reading.

Although overcoming perfectionism can be challenging, it is possible to lighten the load. I have always struggled with perfectionism, and it has cost me plenty. I work daily to become more imperfect! Life is definitely easier with an imperfect mindset.

Let's take a look at Perry's story...

---

1 Brené Brown, *The Gifts of Imperfection: Let Go of Who You Think You're Supposed to Be and Embrace Who You Are* (Center City, MN: Hazeldon Publishing, 2010).

Rock #3: Free Yourself of Perfectionism

Perry was a perfectionist from an early age. He learned that "getting it right" brought him attention and approval. As a child, his perfectionism led him to keep his room clean, ensure his toys were lined up in an exact way, and that he made A's in school. He was the class president, captain of the football team, and voted "most likely to succeed."

After completing his college education, he joined a Fortune 100 company in sales. He was wildly successful and was the top performer in every sales contest he entered. His perfectionism drove him to be #1 at everything he did. He quickly became known throughout the company as the golden boy. The company even produced a video of him talking about how he achieved success in sales. Sales representatives throughout the company viewed this video and tried to emulate him.

Perry climbed the corporate ladder quickly, fueled by his insatiable need for perfection. He felt he had to look, act and be perfect to stay on his pedestal. Beneath the surface, Perry was beginning to crack as the stress and fatigue worsened. He worked long hours, was not taking care of himself, and was shortchanging his relationships. His work took on a life of itself, and he believed perfectionism was the reason behind his success. However, he felt like he was running on a treadmill that never stopped. He began to wonder how long he could continue.

As the Director of Sales, Perry often was the kick-off speaker for large corporate sales events. At one such event, his name was announced, and Perry ran out onto the stage in his usual supercharged manner. Everybody began to clap and cheer. Although Perry was not feeling well, he knew he must "perform." As he began to talk about the successful year they had, Perry began to feel faint. The next thing he knew, the room was spinning, and he collapsed onto the floor. He was quickly surrounded, and an ambulance was called.

At the hospital, Perry expected to hear that he had a heart attack. Numerous tests were run, but the doctors did not find any damage. It turns out Perry had collapsed due to an anxiety attack and exhaustion. This was a wake-up call he could not ignore. He had pushed himself so far that he finally hit the wall. He realized that he needed to face the reality of the impact his perfectionism was having on his life.

With the help of therapy and support from loved ones, Perry began to challenge the unrealistic thoughts that fueled his perfectionism. He realized the cost of maintaining that lifestyle was too high. He had sacrificed his mental and emotional well-being and his relationships with family and friends. He came to understand that mistakes are a normal part of life, and he learned to make mistakes without harsh self-judgment.

He also began to rebuild his life on healthier foundations. He prioritized self-care such as exercise and healthy eating, and he set boundaries to protect himself. His re-connections with his family and friends brought him much joy.

Perry became a stronger, more balanced person as he discovered that true happiness and joy does not come from perfectionism and external achievements. He discovered that true happiness comes from embracing his imperfect, authentic self.

If you are carrying around the rock of perfectionism, you probably have received advice in the past such as "just stop trying to be perfect" or "just lower your expectations." While people mean well, this advice alone is not helpful!

Instead, I want to give you seven specific how-to actions to enable you to begin your journey of becoming more relaxed, and less perfect. Overcoming perfectionism takes time. Remember you are striving for progress, not perfection.

Seven Strategies to Free Yourself of Perfectionism
Below are seven strategies that can help you overcome your perfectionism. Pick several that resonate with you and start with those first. If you stick with it, you will see progress.

Rock #3: Free Yourself of Perfectionism

1. Look at the disadvantages of perfectionism.

Perfectionism can create anxiety, chronic stress, depression, and burnout. It can also lead to low self-esteem and frustration. It can cause procrastination because you can't figure out the "right" way to start, or the project seems overwhelming.

You may even have analysis paralysis, costing you precious time. You realize that it takes you longer than most people to complete a task. Perfectionism can prevent you from leaving your comfort zone and taking risks, leading to missed opportunities. Perfectionism can kill dreams!

YOUR TURN!

Make a list of the disadvantages you are personally experiencing from attempting to be a perfectionist. Write this list on a notecard or put it in your cell phone. Review this list every morning as you begin your day. During the day, if you find yourself beginning to slip back into your perfectionism habit, pull out this list and read it to yourself.

_____

_____

_____

_____

_____

_____

_____

_____

2. Intentionally be imperfect and celebrate mistakes.

Yes, you read this correctly and it is one of my favorite strategies! It forces you to intentionally make a mistake and realize that the "big ugly" is not going to happen.

For example, when I sought help to deal with my perfectionism, here are some of the things I had to do:

- Write the incorrect address on a letter and mail it anyhow.
- Make an intentional typo in an email and send it.
- Make a mistake in a presentation slide and show the slide deck anyway.

I intentionally made mistakes such as these, and nothing bad happened. These were all exaggerated fears in my head. Allowing myself to make intentional mistakes helped reduce my unfounded fear that something awful would occur.

I have come to believe that being perfect is so 1970s/1980s. Back then, we wore the perfect suits and shoes, made perfect presentations, and dared not show our vulnerability. Today, it's a different world. We work at a rapid pace, in a casual environment, and imperfection is more acceptable. Be kind to yourself and accept that imperfection is natural.

YOUR TURN!

List below 3 intentional mistakes you are willing to make in the next week. (It could be anything from forgetting to get all your items at the grocery store, to forgetting to pack several items for your upcoming trip.)

Your Mistake 1:

Your Mistake 2:

Your Mistake 3:

3. Readjust your personal rules.

Perfectionists usually live by a very rigid set of rules. You may recheck your work several times before submitting it or check financial data three times before sending it out, or you may check and recheck a proposal to a customer. Perhaps you have certain rituals for cleaning your house that make it "perfect" or you feel your clothes must be ironed.... the list goes on.

Ask yourself if this is reasonable. Make a decision to reduce your re-checking activities. RESIST and move on. Remember that most mistakes don't create disasters.

That said, I want you to be cognizant about the difference between glass balls and rubber balls. Glass balls are those things that are very important. Perhaps they will be reviewed by upper management, or perhaps it's a compliance rule you must adhere to. These are the ones you want to spend more time on. The rubber balls, which are the majority, are those that are not so important, so decide not to spend time being perfect on these tasks. Remember, glass balls break, rubbers balls simply bounce.

YOUR TURN!

Identify one rule you have that's too rigid. Re-word the rule to be more realistic (e.g. – I am only going to reread my most important emails before I send them.)

The next week, pick another rigid rule to re-write. Keep going each week. Your life will become easier, and you will work faster!

Week 1 "Re-write" one of your rigid rules:

Week 2 "Re-write" a second rigid rule:

Week 3 "Re-write" a third rigid rule:

4. Set time limits.

Set time limits for your tasks and stick to them. This helps you avoid spending excessive time trying to do a task perfectly. Ask yourself what a reasonable amount of time something should take. Set your timer and begin working! Work as quickly as you can, and don't go back and recheck or improve things on this first draft. When the timer rings, move on to something else. Being aware of your time helps you to be more efficient, and helps you accept that sometimes good is good enough.

5. Break tasks into smaller steps.

Procrastination can set in when you are afraid of not doing something perfectly. Procrastination's best friend, indecision, then enters the picture. Indecision stems from the fear of doing something wrong and anticipating dire consequences.

Rock #3: Free Yourself of Perfectionism

To combat this spiraling scenario, break your project into smaller, manageable bits to complete one step at a time. Pick a task and set a date and time to start. Put it on your calendar. Then, do it!!

Two areas where I observe people procrastinating is writing their resume or getting their wills done. People fear not "getting it right" so they stall, sometimes for long periods of time. This can be costly. This approach of breaking it down into smaller tasks can often help people "get going."

When I worked at IBM, I was sometimes assigned a project that seemed massive to me. My close colleague Paul would tell me, "How do you eat an elephant? One bite at a time." And he was right! It was some of the best advice I ever received.

6. Don't major in the minors.

Perfectionism can cause a person to focus on the small details of a project, instead of the bigger picture. It can cause a person to get "tunnel vision."

I worked with someone who was building a curriculum for a large corporation. She spent a great deal of time focusing on such things as the "right" color of blue for the slide deck, the "perfect" font, and special effects. Her results were excellent, but the minor details probably made little difference to the audience. She paid an enormous price for her perfectionism by working untold hours to the detriment of her health and family relationships.

Some strategies for preventing this are to:

- Remember to focus on the bigger picture. This will reduce your urge to be perfect.
- Check-in with yourself periodically and determine if you are getting buried in the details or if you are focusing instead on the substance and meaning you are trying to communicate.

7. Change your self-talk.

Instead of telling yourself that imperfection is unacceptable, tell yourself that:

- Perfectionism is not necessary, nor is it attainable.
- All humans are imperfect.
- Mistakes are a natural part of life.
- Mistakes can teach me far more than a flawless performance.
- I can work much faster without the burden of having to be perfect.
- It is freeing to be an imperfect human being!

Becoming less perfect is challenging, but it is well worth the effort. It also can set you free to explore and try new things.

Rock #4: Stop the People-Pleasing

The only thing wrong with trying to please everyone is that there's always at least one person who will remain unhappy. You.

—*Elizabeth Parker*

Whenever I bring up the topic of people-pleasing, I always see heads nodding. People identify and relate to this "rock" very quickly. I know I do, as it has haunted me since childhood. The problem is that people know they are carrying this burden, but struggle with how to change their behavior.

While being kind and helpful because it brings you joy is a good thing, trying to please everybody can lead to frustration, anxiety, anger, and poor self-care. How many of the following people-pleaser traits do you identify with?

- Strong desire for approval and validation
- Difficulty saying "no"
- Feeling guilty when you do say "no"
- Changing your personality depending on who you are with
- Need validation and praise from others to feel good about yourself
- Preoccupied with what others think of you
- Agree to do things you don't want to do
- Avoid conflict – prefer to not rock the boat
- Tell people you are sorry, even if it is not your fault
- Never have time for yourself because you are always putting others' needs first
- Need others to like you
- Run all your ideas by someone else first

- Difficulty in expressing your wants and feelings
- Feeling responsible for how others feel

If you said yes to some or all of the above signs, you may struggle with people-pleasing tendencies.

Merriam-Webster dictionary defines a *people-pleaser* as "a person who has an emotional need to please others often at the expense of his or her own needs and desires."

The "emotional need" called out in this definition gives us insight into the root cause of people-pleasing. In order to stop this behavior, it is helpful to look at some of these root causes. There are a number of factors that might play a role; they are often complex and intertwined. Here are some of the key factors:

- Childhood experiences
  Many develop people-pleasing behavior in childhood, in response to family dynamics. This can include growing up in a family that avoided conflict or had a lot of conflict, having an emotionally unavailable parent or a parent whose love was conditional, experiencing abuse, or having a parent with addiction or emotional issues. Children growing up in these environments may have developed people-pleasing as a coping mechanism to avoid conflict or earn a parent's love and approval.

- Poor self-esteem
  People with poor self-esteem have a need for external validation and approval from others to feel good about themselves. They feel doing things for others will lead to approval and acceptance.

- Insecurity
  People-pleasers may also feel insecure about their "place in the pack." They might worry that others will not like them if they don't go the extra mile to make them happy.

Rock #4: Stop the People-Pleasing

- Fear of rejection or abandonment
  Many people-pleasers feel that if they do not please others they may be rejected or abandoned. This fear drives them to go above and beyond to please others and avoid conflict. They want to be needed, well-liked, appreciated, and useful.

- Past experiences
  Having experienced painful or traumatic experiences can also trigger people-pleasing. Perhaps a person has experienced a painful divorce and now goes overboard to please the new spouse in an effort to prevent another painful experience. People who have experienced abuse may work hard to please others so that they don't trigger more abusive behavior.

All these situations create an environment ripe for not feeling safe to say no or disagree. Thus, the people pleaser continues to please and say "yes," resulting in a lack of taking care of their own needs, health, and joy.

Oprah Winfrey tells another story about her childhood in her and Dr. Bruce Perry's book *What Happened to You?* Oprah shares a story about how being "whupped" regularly as a child by her grandmother led her to become a people pleaser.

In that day and age, it was acceptable for caregivers to spank children as a method of discipline. I too grew up in that era.

Oprah shares her story of going to the well behind their house to pump water, as their house didn't have inside plumbing. As she went back to the house, Oprah twirled her fingers in the water. From the window, her grandmother observed Oprah doing this. When she asked Oprah if she had been playing in the water, Oprah said "no." Her grandmother was enraged. Not only was it their drinking water, but Oprah had lied. Her grandmother "whupped" her so hard that her flesh welted. Oprah went on to share that she was beaten for the slightest reasons including breaking a glass or spilling water, and even for not being quiet enough. Oprah quickly

Toss the Rocks and Get on With It!

understood that keeping her mouth shut was the best way to avoid punishment and pain.

Due to the long-term impact of being "whupped," Oprah turned into a world-class people pleaser for most of her life. Although she experienced abuse and trauma as a child, she has been able to move forward and form loving quality relationships with many people.[1]

There is hope for all of us. Instead of ignoring our past and the resulting rocks in our buckets, we need to understand the impact and make a conscious decision to live the rest of our lives differently.

My dad shared an article with me about people pleasing that helped me when I entered the corporate world. We fondly referred to it as the "monkey article." This article, from the *Harvard Business Review*, is titled "Management Time: Who's Got the Monkey?"[2] and talks about how a manager keeps taking on problems (the monkeys) from his subordinates. By saying things like "Let me think about it and I'll let you know," or "Let me know what I can do to help you," or "Let me hammer out a draft as to how we might solve this problem together," the manager is actually taking on the monkey. It has transferred from the subordinate's back to the manager's back! The manager is slipping further and further behind in his own work, requests from his boss, and system-imposed requirements.

The manager now has so many issues that have been brought to him from his four subordinates that he goes into the office early one Saturday morning to get caught up. He looks out of his window at the nearest green of the golf course, and who does he see? His four subordinates playing golf! That did it. He realized he must change his behavior, and he did. He met with each of his subordinates and established boundaries. He clearly communicated that the subordinate with the problem owns the problem and ultimately has

---

1   *What Happened to You?*, 11–12.
2   William Oncken, Jr. and Donald L. Wass, "Management Time: Who's Got the Monkey?", November-December 1999 issue of *Harvard Business Review*, https://hbr.org/1999/11/management-time-whos-got-the-monkey.

the responsibility to solve it. He worked diligently to ensure that the monkeys did not transfer to his back.

I can so relate to this article from both a business and personal viewpoint. My own people-pleasing behavior has kept me from saying "no" as I tried to please everyone. I wanted to be accepted, valued, liked, and promoted. The "monkey article" really helped me see that people-pleasing and taking on more and more "monkeys" was to my own detriment. I hope this analogy will help you also!

Once I realized that I had a problem with people-pleasing and that it was very difficult for me to say no, I found a class that taught assertiveness training and attended it independent from the company I worked for at the time. It helped me tremendously and gave me tools to be assertive instead of letting things build up and then becoming passive aggressive. There are numerous online courses for assertiveness training, and you may find them helpful.

Let's look at what it may be costing YOU to be a people-pleaser. If you are constantly trying to please other people, odds are, you are not taking good care of your own needs and feelings. You may even lose sight of who you really are as you become a chameleon – doing what you think people want and becoming who you feel others want you to be. You may seem to change with the wind depending on who you are with.

Constant people-pleasing behavior can lead to:

- Anxiety and stress
- Lack of authenticity
- Burnout
- Resentment
- Lack of self-care
- Anger
- Frustration
- Difficulty making decisions
- Stifled personal growth

Are you ready to change? Are you sick and tired of not having time for yourself because you are so busy pleasing others? Are you ready to toss the rock of people-pleasing and set yourself free?

Seven Strategies to Stop the People-Pleasing

1. Start saying "no."
   Tell yourself that it is okay to say no. This is not being selfish; it's taking care of your own needs. My best friend told me recently that she no longer accepts invitations to do something that she doesn't want to do. While I felt this might be impossible for me, I tried it. And it is freeing. Now I have more time to do what I like to do…things that brings me joy and happiness.

2. Realize that "no" is a complete sentence.
   Refrain from trying to explain your "no." Explaining gives the other person a chance to shoot holes in your answer. For example, let's assume you had great plans for a relaxing and restful evening at home. You get a call asking you to go to a movie. You, however, want to stay home! All you need to say is, "I won't be able to go because I have other plans." That's a true statement! You have plans for yourself and your needs. Don't explain! Or, you can simply say, "Thanks for inviting me, but I can't go tonight." If someone asks me to go into more detail, I like to use my twenty-four year old daughter's answer: "It's complicated." Then I change the subject, usually by asking them a question.

3. Set healthy boundaries.
   Setting healthy boundaries can be difficult for people-pleasers, but it is critical for maintaining well-being and peace of mind. You can start by noticing what you are doing. Are you doing things for others or with others that don't bring you joy? Are there things you regret that you said "yes" to? Decide what brings you joy and what doesn't. Make a decision as to what

Rock #4: Stop the People-Pleasing

you will and won't do and communicate these clearly to others. Remember that you are not being selfish. You are finally taking care of your own needs, and you will be a happier person for doing this!

Come up with some phrases you can use. For example, when I started writing this book, I decided that most mornings would be reserved for this activity alone. My friends respected this and knew not to call me until the afternoon. The key was to set the boundary, communicate it, and stick to it.

4. Allow time before responding.

    When someone asks you for a favor or asks you to do something, buy yourself some time. Say something like, "Let me check my calendar and get back to you." Saying "yes" immediately leaves you feeling committed to the event or favor before you have a chance to determine if you really want to do something. Do some soul-searching and decide if it is something that would bring you joy, and if you have time in your calendar without stressing yourself. Don't sacrifice the things that bring you happiness, just to please someone else. Always check your motives.

5. Manage guilt.

    This is a tough one. Sometimes it just seems easier to please the other person instead of feeling guilty about not doing it. The guilt we experience from saying no is complex and multifaceted, rooted in the things we discussed earlier such as fears, past experiences, and beliefs. Deep down, we know that feeling guilty is not healthy and we certainly have noticed that other people say no and don't feel guilty!

    Acknowledge that it is time to change. Be willing to challenge and reframe this negative self-talk about feeling guilty. We are basically telling ourselves that others' needs are more important than our own! This is neither true, nor healthy. Remind yourself that you must first take care of your own needs, and that you can pick and choose what to do for others based on your available time and what brings you joy.

6. Spend time alone.
   When you spend time alone, there is nobody else to please but yourself! This is a great way to fully focus on your own self-care, enabling you to recharge emotionally, physically, and mentally. Think of things that bring you joy and are relaxing. Perhaps it's reading a good book, taking a long bath, burning your favorite candles, cooking your favorite meal, taking a nap, going for a walk, or watching the sunset. This "pause" from the outside world can leave you feeling rested and refreshed. Set a goal and plan to spend some time alone each week, even if it's for a short time. You may find that you want more and more "me" time!

7. Stop asking other people for their opinions.
   Seeking other people's opinions is common for people-pleasers. This could be due to a lack of self-confidence, fear of making the wrong decision, or trying to please someone else. People-pleasers feel a strong need to validate their choices through external sources instead of trusting their own judgement and desires. This is a vicious cycle. Deep down, most of us know what we want. If we ask someone else's opinion, they may pick a different option. Then we have a conundrum. Do we do what makes us happy, or do we acquiesce and take the suggestion of the other person?

   The solution is to trust your own instincts and not ask for opinions to begin with! Your opinions are just as valid as someone else's. Start small with minor decisions such as what to wear or what restaurant to go to for dinner. Communicate clearly, using assertive language such as "I prefer..." or "What I would like to do is ..." State your own opinion first, so that you are not tempted to go with the opinion of the other person.

Rock #4: Stop the People-Pleasing

In conclusion, overcoming people-pleasing can be challenging, but is essential for developing self-confidence, simplifying your life, and gaining more joy in your journey. Be kind to yourself as you begin to break this habit. And remember, YOU matter!

Rock #5: Let Go of Resentments

> *Resentment is like drinking poison and waiting for the other person to die.*
> —*Attributed to Carrie Fisher*

When we hold on to resentments, we are the ones being harmed. As we play the resentment over and over in our minds, we become consumed with anxiety and anger. We are allowing another person to "rent space in our heads" by taking up our time and energy.

The bottom line is that if you are still holding on to resentments, you need to look hard at the impact this is having on your life. Resentments have to do with your PAST. When you hang on to them, you are allowing your past to negatively impact your present and your future.

Resentments can be triggered by horrendous events such as abuse to an innocent child, heartbreaking events such as divorce or broken relationships, or workplace issues that cut deep into values such as trust or broken dreams. Whatever the trigger, they are gut wrenching and leave deep scars.

Sometimes one of these resentments may pop into our heads and we revel in our anger and may even hate the alleged perpetrator. We may discuss it with a friend who joins our cause and curses the aggressor along with us, making us feel even more justified in our anger. We may spend time thinking about how to seek revenge.

The problem is that mourning or reliving the past keeps us stuck and can prevent new doors from opening. As Helen Keller said:

> *When one door of happiness closes, another opens, but often we look so long at the closed door that we do not see the one which has been opened for us.*
> —*Helen Keller*

Rock #5: Let Go of Resentments

For example, how many of you are still mourning that failed relationship?

Are these emotions keeping you from seeing the new doors opening for potential new relationships?

Or are you still so angry at your past business partner that you are missing new opportunities?

At some point, we need to STOP and ask ourselves if this is serving us well. The person it is hurting is you! Odds are the person that hurt you has gone on with their life and is not thinking about you. But you are thinking about them...and it may be hijacking your life. Each time you play it over and over in your mind, it is negatively impacting you emotionally, physically, and spiritually. It repeatedly makes you feel victimized and hurt.

So, what does it cost you to hold on to your hurt and resentments? I came across the following quote which sums it up clearly:

> The moment you start to resent a person, you become his slave. He controls your dreams, absorbs your digestion, robs you of your peace of mind and goodwill, and takes away the pleasure of your work. He ruins your religion and nullifies your prayers. You cannot take a vacation without his going along. He destroys your freedom of mind and hounds you wherever you go. There is no way to escape the person you resent. He is with you when you are awake. He invades your privacy when you sleep. He is close beside you when you drive your car and when you are on the job. You can never have efficiency or happiness. He influences even the tone of your voice. He requires you to take medicine for indigestion, headaches, and loss of energy. He even steals your last moment of consciousness before you go to sleep. So, if you want to be a slave, harbor your resentments!
>
> — *Attributed to Elizabeth Kenny*

It makes no logical sense to hold on to your resentments! People can, and do, get over them. It takes determination, faith, and the acknowledgement that letting go of the resentment is a CHOICE. It all starts within each of us. Make a decision to toss the rock of resentment and set yourself free!

YOUR TURN!

Before we dive into the HOW to toss the rock of resentment, I want you to do some introspection. Think of your own resentment(s) and ask yourself these questions:

1. Who am I resentful toward?

2. What is the cause for each of the above resentments? (What did this person do to me)?

3. Why am I holding on to these resentments?

4. How are they impacting my life?

5. Who is it hurting?

Seven Strategies for Letting Go of Resentments

1. Talk to someone.

Talk to a trusted friend, family member, pastor, or mentor. Keeping your resentments bottled up inside is not healthy. Simply talking about it may bring some relief and clarity to the situation. The other person may be able to offer you a new perspective or plan to help you get unstuck, and enable you to let go of your resentments.

2. Choose forgiveness.

To forgive is to set a prisoner free and discover that prisoner was you.
—*Lewis B. Smedes, author and theologian*

If you have a resentment, it means that you have not forgiven the other person. I believe that forgiveness is the #1 antidote to resentment. I love this strategy because not only does it work, but it is an action we can take on our own, without anybody else's agreement or interaction. It is a gift to ourselves because it frees us from resentment. Forgiveness is not so much about the other person's actions as it is about your own serenity.

You may be saying to yourself that there is no way you can forgive those who have hurt you, wronged you, or abused you. But I am asking you to keep an open mind. Forgiveness is for you, not the other person. It has the power to set you free.

An extraordinary example of forgiveness comes from the life of Corrie ten Boom. She was a Dutch Christian who, along with her family, helped hundreds of Jews escape the Nazi Holocaust by hiding them in their home. They were eventually discovered and arrested by the Nazis. Cory, along with her father and sister, Betsie, were sent to concentration camps. Corrie's father died soon after the arrest. Corrie and her sister endured unspeakable suffering in the Ravensbruck concentration camp.

Amid these horrors, Betsie remained steadfast in her faith and encouraged Cory to forgive her captors. Sadly, Betsie died in the concentration camp. When Corrie was released, she decided to carry on her sister's legacy of forgiveness. She traveled the world sharing her story of survival and the power of forgiveness.

An incredible act of forgiveness came when one of the guards from her concentration camp showed up when Corrie was speaking at a church in Munich. At the close of the service, he came forward to meet her. She froze. She recognized him although he had no idea who she was. With incredible strength and courage, she reached out and shook his hand as she told him that she forgave him.

Corrie's story takes my breath away. The resentments in my life pale in comparison to what she experienced. It shows that each of us can forgive and move forward if we make the choice and put it into action.

As you work on forgiving those who you have a resentment against, remember that does not mean you are condoning the other person's actions. It is about tossing the rock and releasing yourself from the burden.

Sometimes the person you need to forgive is yourself. You may resent yourself for past mistakes or for your perceived weaknesses. Here again, you are only hurting yourself. Forgive yourself and move forward onto a positive path.

3. Look at both sides.

Try to see the situation from the other person's perspective. I know this can be difficult, especially if your level of anger is high. However, there are always two sides to every story. The other person also had thoughts, feelings, and motivation for their actions. Understanding their struggles and thought processes can help you see things more clearly.

This has personally worked for me. Remember my story about my college sweetheart who broke my heart? I blamed him for years because HE was the one who cheated on me. HE was the reason we didn't get married. HE was the one who broke my trust and abandoned me. I was clearly the victim, or so I thought for 10 years until I finally looked at MY part.

Rock #5: Let Go of Resentments

I was the one who could not commit to marriage due to deep seated fears. At the time, I was not even cognizant as to why I had this fear. I had not processed that part of my past. Finally looking at his side, I can only imagine the rejection he may have felt, not to mention the disappointment. I am sure he was bewildered and confused.

Because I could then see my part, the resentment vanished. It was almost magical. When we open ourselves up to different perspectives, it's as if the fog disappears and we can see clearly, perhaps for the first time.

I believe that usually the person that caused you pain is not trying to intentionally hurt you. They are often just trying to save themselves, or they are out of touch with the impact their actions are having on you.

Forgiveness is not easy, but it is necessary for your own peace of mind.

4. Talk to the other person.

This strategy can be dicey, and I suggest you carefully analyze if it will work in your situation.

You must be willing to:

- Listen – this is more important than talking! You do not learn anything by talking, but you can learn a lot by "seeking to understand."
- Carefully state your feelings without blaming the other person. You must use "I" statements vs. "You" statements. Don't say things like "You never help me with the kids," or "You never help me around the house" or "You don't appreciate all that I do." Instead, use "I" statements. Say things like
"I am feeling overwhelmed and would love to have more support with doing things for the kids and the household. What ideas do you have?" Or, if you feel unappreciated, say something like "I am not feeling very appreciated. I think I just

need to hear it verbalized more often." The wording of that last sentence is important. You are saying what you want the other person to do versus putting them down for what they are not doing. Say what you want a person to do, not what you don't want.

- Write down what you want to say and review it to ensure you are using "I" statements. Once you go into "You do this" or "You do that," the other person will most likely get defensive, and the battle is on! Don't go there! Remember, you want this person to work WITH you.
- Remain calm. Once you lose your composure, the conversation can go south. Remind yourself that you are trying to stay in the game and keep the conversation going in a positive direction.

It may not always be possible to have a conversation with the other person. Perhaps the person will not even speak to you or perhaps the person is dead.

5. Write a letter.

Another effective strategy is to write a letter to the other person. You do not have to mail the letter. In fact, if it is an "angry" letter, it is best left unsent.

I know people who have written these letters and gone to a graveside and read them. They say that it relieves the resentment, and they are finally able to let go. I've heard the same from people who have written letters, then torn them up and thrown them out. This symbolizes the release of the resentment.

A friend of mine, Susie, discovered an unresolved childhood trauma via Eye Movement Desensitization and Reprocessing (EMDR) therapy. She had repressed the trauma and did not even consciously remember it. The trauma was that she had been sexually abused repeatedly by her grandfather, and her mother had not protected her. As these memories came back, Susie was overcome by emotions, especially the anger and resentment toward her mother. It took her one and a half years to process everything, during which time she avoided her mother. Meanwhile, her mother's health declined, and she was moved to a nursing home. Susie wrote a letter to her mother expressing her hurt and anger, but she never mailed it. When Susie received a call from her brother that her mother was near the end, Susie caught a flight and went to the nursing home. Although Susie's mother was in an unconscious state, she read the letter to her mother, told her that she remembered the abuse, and that she forgave her. It was an act of cleansing, and Susie was able to forgive and move forward with her life.

6. Surrender and move on.
Perhaps you are in a relationship where the other person is the way they are, and they are not willing to change. Or you are in a work situation which is toxic and you have no control over it. Or someone has treated you unfairly in a business deal but has no desire to communicate with you. You have exhausted all your strategies and resources, and nothing helps. You are emotionally drained and exhausted. What then?

It may be time for surrender. Let it go! Make a decision to stop trying to analyze the resentment or create change. Accept that you are not able to change other people. You can only change yourself.

7. Seek professional help.
If you have tried the above strategies, and nothing has helped, you may want to join a support group or see a counselor. A professional can help you dig deeper into your emotions and past with the goal of helping you release the resentments and find internal peace.

Resentment is a rock in your bucket that is far too heavy to carry around for the rest of your life. Toss the rock, and free your soul. Remember that it takes time and determination to let go of resentments. Be patient and kind to yourself and celebrate small victories.

Rock #6: Overcome Addictions

Addiction is a strong word. Perhaps you have an addiction, or maybe you are at the stage where you are abusing a substance, or self-medicating, but not yet out of control. Or perhaps you are engaging in activities such as porn, gambling, or have an eating disorder. Maybe you are controlling it for now. But it is a slippery slope. Please take the time to read this chapter so that you fully understand the consequences of continuing the behavior. If this does not pertain to you personally, I bet you know someone who does have an issue. Perhaps you can reach out a helping hand.

In this chapter, we are talking about all types of addictions including:

- Alcohol
- Drugs
- Eating disorders
- Sex
- Gambling
- Shopping
- Porn
- Nicotine
- Working
- Exercising

People with addiction issues find it easier to DENY having an addiction than to get honest with themselves. If they are honest, they may have to change. Giving up their addiction can be scary. People with addiction issues feel their addiction, be it overeating, retail therapy, drugs, alcohol, or something else are their best friends. They feel unable to cope with life without their "fix." Thus, they work hard to keep the addiction a secret, or they are in total denial about their addiction. It is not uncommon for a person to "stretch the truth" when asked by a doctor about their amount of alcohol or drug use. Or to lie to a loved one in order to avoid scrutiny.

Addiction is a symptom of an underlying problem such as fear, anxiety, loneliness, resentments, or something that is not working in their lives. The addictive behavior is a way to "escape" these feelings. It is a way to "numb out" or an attempt to make oneself feel better, even though that relief is temporary. As soon as the "fix" wears off, the pain returns. Long-term, it never solves anything. Ironically, not only does the underlying issue remain, but the person may feel guilty about the over-indulgence.

It's a vicious cycle. For example, a person may be feeling stressed, so they binge drink. Next, they feel hungover and are mad at themselves or ashamed. Then the painful emotions come back, and the person is drinking again to avoid the real problem and to feel better.

The sad part is that once someone gives into the obsession, they want more of it. When they have "just one" of a trigger food, drink, or activity, they break out into "not-enoughness." The old saying "One is one too many and one more is never enough" is so true for someone with an addiction. It's like telling oneself lies such as:

- One piece of candy won't hurt.

- I'll only have one drink.

- I'll just go shopping one time this week.

- Watching 10 minutes of porn won't hurt anybody.

In essence, it is an attempt to anesthetize one's feelings. The truth is that only by feeling and addressing the rocks that haunt us, will we become free and happy. The problem is within us, and nothing on the outside can fix us. We must feel and walk through the pain vs trying to escape.

One of the reasons people don't get help is shame. They feel they are all alone in their pain, and that others would look down on them if they knew the truth. Shame keeps the person in isolation. The reality is that you are not alone.

According to the 2022 United States National Survey on Drug Use and Health (NSDUH):

- 48.7 million (17.3%) of Americans (aged 12 and older) battled a substance use disorder in the past year.
- 29.5 million (10.5%) of Americans 12 and older had an <u>alcohol use disorder</u> (AUD) in the past year. This is about 1 in 10 people.
- 27.2 million (9.7%) of Americans aged 12 or older had a Drug Use Disorder (DUD) in the past year. This is also about 1 in 10 people.

Keep in mind that often the addiction is not initially the issue, but instead a "bad solution" to temporarily deal with pain. But the cycle is endless. As soon as the "fix" wears off, the pain returns. Only by dealing with our core issues can we begin to improve our lives and be free.

I speak from experience. I was working crazy hours, had a three-year-old, and was the main bread winner. Layoffs were prevalent, and I was stressed out that my job would be next. As people were laid off, the work did not go away, but instead, was piled on those who were still there. To cope, I began to drink more frequently. It numbed the pain and helped me work late at night… sometimes until 1:00 or 2:00 am. Along with this lifestyle came sleep deprivation. I was trying to keep up appearances on the outside, while inside, my ship was sinking.

I dared not tell anyone how much I was drinking. It was my crutch, my "friend," and I thought I would be unable to cope without the alcohol to soothe me. But we all know where this story goes. I was

Rock #6: Overcome Addictions

not addressing the real problems. Nothing was changing. I was so trapped in fear that I could not see any options to make my life less stressful. I certainly could have used a personal coach at that point in my life, but I didn't reach out for help for a long time. Fortunately, I did face my issues. Once I quit drinking, I was able to address the underlying problems and become free.

My point is that it's a CHOICE! When we deny that an addiction exists, we can't change it. Only when we get honest with ourselves can we enact change.

Addictions are characterized by compulsive engagement in a behavior in spite of adverse consequences. The "cost" of hanging on to addictions include:

- Health Issues
  These can include damage to the brain, liver, and heart; increased risk of HIV/AIDS through unsafe sex or sharing needles; and psychological problems such as depression and anxiety.
- Relationship Damage
  Addictions can lead to troubled relationships with family, friends, and co-workers. These may result from behavioral changes in the user or from lying about their addiction, where they have been, or why they are spending so much money. This leads to broken trust and conflicts. It can also lead to divorces and child custody issues.
- Work Issues
  Addictions can cause declining performance, increased absenteeism, conflict with co-workers and managers, loss of employment, and difficulty in finding employment.
- Problems at School
  Addictions or over-indulgences can result in decreased academic performance, lack of motivation to excel, distractions, and loss of financial aid.

- Financial Difficulties
  Spending money to support an addiction, especially a drug habit, gambling, or shopping addiction can be significant. It can lead to debt, financial instability, and even bankruptcy.
- Legal Issues
  Legal issues associated with substance abuse or other criminal activities include arrests, fines, prosecution, jail time, and probation. These legal ramifications can snowball and affect other areas of one's life such as job loss, financial strain and broken relationships.
- Overdose or suicide
  We are all too familiar with the number of deaths caused by addictions, especially with drugs and alcohol. We hear of people overdosing and dying, fatal accidents, and suicide. Continued substance abuse increases the odds of tragic outcomes.

Think hard about these costs and ask yourself if it is worth it. There truly is a better path forward.

Let's look at Penny's story and how she turned her life around.

PENNY'S STORY

My father was a very strict man and was emotionally absent. He expected perfection from me, and I was never good enough. When I brought home 2 A++ and 3 A's, he pointed to the A's and said, "What happened?"

As a child, I always remember feeling like I was on the outside looking in. I vividly remember, in the fourth grade, standing on a hill at the playground. I was looking at the other girls feeling like I did not fit in, that I was not smart enough, or pretty enough. I felt my clothes were shabby, and I turned all these feeling inward. These became the rocks in my bucket that I carried most of my life.

Rock #6: Overcome Addictions

I started drinking at 17 on Saturday nights. By the time I was in college, I drank to get drunk. After college, I married my high school sweetheart who drank like I did! He quickly climbed the corporate ladder, and I was attending business dinners and functions at age 24. As in my childhood, I never felt good enough when attending these events. I drank to fit in. It gave me the ease and comfort I was missing.

When my children were young, I was very cautious about drinking around them…for a while. By the time they were both in elementary school, I was drinking at 9 am. As the bus picked them up, I would pop my first beer. I did this because I had severe anxiety, and I didn't know why. Beer quelled the anxiety. It was my coping mechanism and I believed it helped me live.

I drank beer until my husband got home at 6:00. Then we would have cocktails together. It was a way of life for me, and I never thought that I might have a drinking problem. For me, I was solving my anxiety problem by numbing out.

After about 22 years, I decided to see a psychiatrist for my overwhelming anxiety. He put me on benzo tranquilizers which helped somewhat, but I quickly got addicted to them!

After eight years of tranquilizers, mixed with alcohol, I finally agreed to check-in to a treatment center to get off the prescription pills. My first day of treatment, I had a huge aha. I realized for the first time, that I was an alcoholic. The thought had never crossed my mind. I had been in utter and total denial.

To get clean and sober, I had to look at the "rocks in my bucket." I joined a 12-step program, and only then could I look at my past and see where I had developed many negative and damaging thoughts about myself.

Through my 12-step program, I was able to take each hurtful rock, deal with it emotionally, and see it for what it was. Previously, I had internalized everything – my fears, anxieties, and lack of self-confidence. I had kept everything a secret.

I made the choice to put down my alcohol and drugs and live life on life's terms. I decided I would no longer let my past ruin my present or future. Once I walked through the pain, the anxiety went away. Today I live a grateful life of peace and contentment.

Penny realized her life was not working and made the CHOICE to change. This decision is available to everyone.

Seven Strategies for Overcoming Addictions

1. Ask yourself, "What am I trying to *not* feel?"
   Think back to the rocks you listed that are banging around in your bucket. Decide to address these directly instead of drinking, drugging, eating, shopping, gambling, etc. in an attempt to not feel the pain.
   The addiction may help temporarily but it never does for the long-term. Acknowledge this and face your issues head on.

2. Find healthier ways to feed your feelings.
   In Step Two: Envision You Ideal Life, you did an exercise on "Things I Love Doing." Look back at this exercise and review those things that bring you happiness and joy. Perhaps it's a massage, reading a book, burning delicious smelling candles, a long bath, going on a walk, talking to a friend, taking a nap, or something else. Just do something that makes you happy. When you have the urge to drink, drug or participate in any addictive behavior, try one of these healthier activities instead.

3. Practice self-care.
   Give yourself full permission to take care of yourself first. Getting regular exercise, eating healthy, getting adequate sleep, and setting realistic goals can improve your overall well-being and make you less vulnerable to addictive behaviors.

Rock #6: Overcome Addictions

4. Talk to a trusted friend.
   Pick someone who is a confidante, non-judgmental, and a good listener. This could be a good friend, a pastor, a personal coach, your significant other, or someone else. The point is to be totally honest and release your "secret." Remember that secrets keep you sick. Let go of the secret, and its power over you will diminish.

5. Seek professional help.
   There are therapists, counselors, and addiction specialists who can help you understand your underlying issues and provide you with a personalized plan.

6. Join a support group.
   Many people go directly to a support group. Because AA is exclusive to those with an alcohol addiction, a number of other programs were formed to support those recovering from other addictive disorders. Some of these programs are:
   AA – Alcoholics Anonymous
   CA – Cocaine Anonymous
   CMA – Crystal Meth Anonymous
   GA – Gamblers Anonymous
   HA - Heroin Anonymous
   MA – Marijuana Anonymous
   NA – Narcotics Anonymous
   NicA – Nicotine Anonymous
   OA – Overeaters Anonymous
   OLGA – Online Gamers Anonymous
   PA – Pills Anonymous – prescription pill addiction
   SAA – Sex Addicts Anonymous
   In these support groups, you will find that you are not alone. This community will allow you to be open and honest and will provide you with a path to recovery. The framework is based

on the original 12 Steps of Alcoholics Anonymous, which involves admitting powerlessness over the addiction, surrendering, seeking help from a higher power, determining character defects, making amends, and working toward personal growth and recovery.

7. Check into a rehab center.
These can be outpatient or inpatient or in a residential treatment center. They provide supervised programs to help stop addictions and gain tools to live a heathy life.

Bottom line, it is up to you to make the decision to surrender and gain a life that is joyous, happy, and free. I have met numerous people in recovery who are living a life of joy and serenity. There is laughter, camaraderie, compassion, and fun! You have been thrown a lifeline. All you need to do is grab hold of it and take action.

PART 3

THE TIME TO ACT IS NOW!

I trust that you now have a good grasp on your current situation, the vision of your ideal life, and the rocks that are getting in your way. Now is the time to ACT! Don't put this book down! You are at a pivotal point. It is the doing, the action, that can change the trajectory of your life.

Sometimes we avoid this ACTION step by clinging to our comfort zones, stating such things as:

- "When I get my house in order, I'll take on these tasks."
- "When I lose some weight, it will be easier for me to exercise."
- "When my child graduates from high school, I will look at changing jobs."
- "When my child graduates from college, I will look at why my marriage is no longer fulfilling."

Often we make excuses because we fear change. This is common, but the excuses keep us stuck. Remember the frog in the boiling water? Is that you? Does the water just keep getting hotter?

It's time to stop making excuses. It's time to walk through the fear of change. The time to focus on YOU is NOW!

Step Six

Develop Your Personal Action Plan

This step is the game changer! It's where you close the gap between where you are now and where you want to be.

A bold action plan will propel you out of your comfort zone and into action. It will take you out of your self-doubts and focus you on the excitement of moving your life forward.

You are no longer stuck. You know that your past negative experiences and beliefs do not define your future. You are now in motion, and nothing can stop you unless you let it.

First, we will begin by summarizing what you have learned about yourself during this journey. It is important to have a big picture visual. Go back to the previous steps and write down the following:

MY CURRENT SITUATION: (as listed at the end of STEP 1)

_____

_____

_____

_____

_____

_____

_____

_____

_____

MY IDEAL LIFE (as listed at the end of STEP 2)

ROCKS IN MY BUCKET (As listed at the end of Step 3)

Next, you will write your ACTION PLAN. There are numerous formats for action plans, but I believe in keeping it simple. I also believe in the "Power of 3." For our action plans, we will list 3 categories: Goals, Tasks and Time Frames.

Each goal should be a "SMART" goal. SMART is a framework for setting goals. It is widely used in both personal and professional settings. The acronym stands for:

S= Specific	Well-defined goals that are clear and specific. You state exactly what you are trying to achieve.
M= Measurable	Make sure you can measure your success. Use metrics or date targets.
A= Achievable	Ensure that goals are realistic and genuinely attainable.
R = Relevant	Ensure that goals are relevant to YOU.
T= Time-Bound	Assign an end date. Give yourself a deadline.

Your action plan does not have to be perfect, and it will keep evolving. The objective is to get it on paper now and start working your plan. Please feel free to dive right in, or you can first refer to the action plan example below.

Tommy's **CURRENT SITUATION:**

- Not happy with my job. No longer excited, just tolerating it
- Fear of public speaking, which is holding me back in my career
- Have a "rock" of people-pleasing, which leaves me with little time for things that I enjoy
- Physically out of shape – not exercising, overweight
- No longer spending quality time with my wife, so the romance is waning

Tommy's **IDEAL LIFE:**

- Land a new job that is exciting and provides career and financial growth
- Able to "take the stage" and present my ideas and proposals clearly and confidently
- Able to say "no" to people when it is not something I want to do
- Lose 10 pounds and have a body that is strong and lean
- Re-energize the romance in my marriage

Tommy's **ROCKS IN HIS BUCKET:**

- Fear of change
- Insecurity
- Fear of public speaking
- People-pleasing
- Lack of self-care
- Intimacy issues

TOMMY'S ACTION PLAN
June 3

GOALS/TASKS	COMPLETION DATE *
GOAL: Land a new job that I would enjoy and provides growth	9/10

GOALS/TASKS	COMPLETION DATE *
TASKS:	
Update resume	6/21
Update LinkedIn profile	6/28
Create a compelling cover letter	6/30
Network with people in desired industry. Be seen!	Ongoing
Research companies that align with my skill set	7/5
Apply for jobs and complete at least 3 interviews	8/2
Continue applying and interviewing for jobs	Ongoing
GOAL: Overcome fear of public speaking	10/15
TASKS:	
Research tips and techniques for public speaking	7/12
Join a group, such as Toastmasters, that helps people with public speaking	7/19
Develop a presentation I would like to give	7/26
Rehearse my speech with a few friends and ask for honest feedback; video my presentation	7/31
Watch the video of my presentation	8/1
Rehearse in front of a mirror	8/2
Make a presentation to a small audience	8/9
Continue to make presentations	Ongoing
GOAL: Improve my physical well-being	11/15
TASKS:	
Join a health club; get a strength assessment and exercise plan	6/14
Participate in 2 strength training classes per week	ongoing

Toss the Rocks and Get on With It!

GOALS/TASKS	COMPLETION DATE *
Complete 2 cardio classes per week (or walk 2-3 miles)	ongoing
Develop a balanced meal plan for weight loss	6/21
Track food intake daily using an app such as MyFitnessPal	6/21 & ongoing
Lose 10 pounds	9/15
GOAL: Spend more quality time with my wife	Now and ongoing
TASKS:	
Brainstorm with my wife about ideas for fun, quality activities we can do together	6/7
Have a date night once a week	Ongoing
Surprise wife with one gift per month	by the end of each month
Have dinner together every night with no electronic devices	Daily
GOAL: Reduce my people-pleasing tendencies	12/15
TASKS:	
Seek therapy to determine where this "rock" came from and how to let it go	6/28
Write down, for 3 weeks, each time I say "Yes" to something I don't really want to do	6/7 - 6/21
Set boundaries and prioritize my personal needs	7/12
Practice saying "No"	Ongoing

Develop Your Personal Action Plan

*Completion dates are sequential *within* each goal. However, multiple tasks from multiple goals should be worked on concurrently.

YOUR TURN!

Write your personal bold action plan below:

ACTION PLAN FOR: _____

DATE: _____

GOALS/TASKS	COMPLETION DATE
GOAL:	
TASKS:	
GOAL:	
TASKS:	

Toss the Rocks and Get on With It!

GOALS/TASKS	COMPLETION DATE
GOAL:	
TASKS:	
GOAL:	
TASKS:	

Develop Your Personal Action Plan

GOALS/TASKS	COMPLETION DATE
GOAL:	
TASKS:	

Be sure to celebrate your successes! Reward yourself with something fun and enjoyable when you accomplish a task or goal. You need to update your action plan on a regular basis to keep yourself moving forward. Congratulations on taking this big step! And here's to your bright future, free of rocks and full of JOY!

Conclusion

As we come to the end of *Toss the Rocks and Get On With It!*, let's reflect on the journey we have taken together. Using the six-step process, you assessed your current situation and envisioned your ideal life of joy. You acknowledged the gap and chose to determine how to get from your current to your ideal life.

You became aware of the negative rocks you gathered from your past, and you evaluated the cost of hanging on to them.

You made a choice not to let past rocks such as fears, insecurity, self-doubt, perfectionism, people-pleasing, resentments, and addictions define your future. These rocks have weighed you down for far too long, hindering your ability to fully embrace life and experience true joy.

You learned strategies on how to toss these rocks. By doing this, you reclaimed your power and right to joy. Lastly, you developed a bold action plan to live your best life, full of joy, serenity and happiness.

Your past is a chapter in your story, but it is not the entire book. You are the author of your present and future, and you hold the pen. Every day is a fresh start, and an opportunity to choose joy. There will be times when old fears resurface, or new problems arise. When this happens, return to the six-steps you've learned, reassess, and continue to let go. Be patient and compassionate with yourself.

According to an unknown author:

"In the end, we only regret the chances we didn't take, the relationships we were afraid to have, and the decisions we waited too long to make."

You have the power within you to overcome any obstacle, to release any rock and to live a life filled with joy, peace, and happiness. Believe in your strength to transform your life, and let that belief guide you in every step you take.

As you finish this book, I encourage you to keep moving forward, to keep identifying and tossing your rocks, and to keep choosing joy. There is a bright future, and it's yours to create. You have more strength and power than you think. So, get on with it - embrace the freedom that comes with letting go and step confidently into the life of joy that you deserve.

Thank you for sharing this journey with me. I wish you all the best and hope your future is filled with peace, joy and boundless opportunities.

—Donna